Advertising: Industry in Peril

An Insider Exposes Advertising's Ten Fundamental
Problems and Reveals the Secrets to Overcoming Them

John Michelet

🔥 Olympian
Publishing
Tigard, Oregon

ISBN–10:0-9778982-0-2
ISBN–13:978-0-97778982-0-6

Library of Congress Control Number: 2006928962

Michelet, John.
    Advertising : industry in peril : an insider exposes
advertising's ten fundamental problems and reveals the
secrets to overcoming them / John Michelet. -- 1st ed.
    p. cm.
    Includes bibliographical references and index.
    LCCN 2006928962
    ISBN-13: 978-0-9778982-0-6
    ISBN-10: 0-9778982-0-2

    1. Advertising--United States.   I. Title.

HF5813.U6M525 2006   659.1'0973
                       QBI06-600308

Edited by Richard Speer and Robert Michelet
Design and Cover by Quavondo Nguyen
Photography by Kristina Wright

ACKNOWLEDGEMENTS

I want to honor the people who have made major contributions to my life and my understanding of advertising, and have ultimately had a hand in writing this book. First, of course, praise and thanks to Jesus Christ for His love, grace, mercy, patience, and the gifts He so generously gives. My grateful thanks to:

My parents, John and Vivian, for going the extra mile for my brother Bob and me, and for teaching us the importance of excellence in anything you do.

My brother Bob for his love, support, hard work, ideas, keen insights and generous assistance.

My wife Anne, my daughter Lindsay, my son Erik for their love, support, patience and understanding.

Jocelyn, a very special person and the best business partner anyone could want.

Linda, Jack, Nancy in San Diego, Claudia, Nancy in Portland, Kathy, Don, Keith, Quavondo, Kristina and Richard.

LIST OF VISUALS

Our thanks to the National Turkey Federation, Toyota Motor Sales and J & J Consumer Companies, Inc. for allowing us to include their ads in this book.

The following trademarks appear in this book: Turkey the perfect protein, RoC Retinol Correxion, and We Keep our Promises.

Although the author and publisher have exhaustively researched all sources to ensure the accuracy and completeness of the information contained in this book, we assume no responsibility for errors, inaccuracies, omissions or any other inconsistency herein. Any slights against people or organizations are unintentional.

Attention colleges and universities, corporations, and writing and publishing organizations: Quantity discounts are available on bulk purchases of this book for educational training purposes, fund-raising, or gift giving. For information, contact Olympian Publishing, 13500 SW Pacific Highway, PMB 522, Tigard, OR 97223, (503) 590-0303.

WHO, WHY, AND WHAT

WHO SHOULD READ THIS BOOK?

I wrote this book for you:

- If you work for an organization that advertises, and your title contains the word "advertising," "marketing," "marcom," "communications," or "research."

- If you are you a manager, owner, board member or anyone else who reviews and approves advertising for your organization. You owe it to your cohorts to read this so you can provide the enlightened leadership for which you get the big bucks.

- If you work in the account service group or creative department of an advertising agency. You need to read it so you can do what's best for your clients and your agency. Read it so you can maximize your competitive edge, and make your competitors look uninformed and unprepared.

- If you are a media salesperson, especially if you write ads for your clients. It will greatly increase the chances of your clients having success with you.

- If you like getting the inside scoop on issues and trends of major importance to our economy.

- If you are looking for something to read on your next flight. You will find it surprising, intriguing and enlightening.

WHO IS THE AUTHOR?

In my thirty-five years in advertising, I have accumulated an extraordinary amount of knowledge and perspective on advertising, and a passion for helping people do it right.

Armed with a BA in Sociology from the University of Oregon and an MBA in Marketing from the Stanford University Graduate School of Business, I have had an unusually broad range of experience in advertising and marketing.

I have worked on both the advertiser and advertising agency sides of the business, working at large and small agencies, for large and small advertisers. In an ad agency, you seldom work on both the creative and account service teams. I have been blessed with successful experience as an account manager, copywriter and creative director.

On the advertiser side, I have been a Marketing Manager and Vice President of Marketing for consumer products companies. As a marketer, I won the Pride award for national marketing program excellence in the home furnishings industry.

I have won forty-two awards in national and regional creative competitions, including national first place winners in TV and radio categories. Finally, for over 20 years, I have been privileged to spread my passion for advertising excellence as an Adjunct Instructor of Advertising in the Business School of Portland State University.

It is now my pleasure to share with you my insights and strategies for success.

WHAT IT SAYS

This book has two parts. The first part is diagnostic, defining the serious and widespread problems in the advertising business. The second part is prescriptive, identifying the actions that should be taken to address the problems.

Part One - Problems

The first part is designed to give a wake up call to the slumbering advertising business, to alert it that the business has serious problems that need to be dealt with now. This is by far the largest part, since it is important that advertisers and ad agencies alike realize there are major problems, and understand the causes and interrelationships of these problems.

The inability of the advertising industry to satisfy either consumers or advertisers is due to ten related internal problems. The first part of the book identifies and analyzes these ten major problems that result in most advertising done in this country being ineffective and pretty useless.

Don't Expect Proof

I can't present statistics to prove that most of the advertising done in this country is ineffective. For one reason, there is nothing to measure. There is no commonly accepted definition or measurement of effectiveness.

People in the industry and the general public alike often equate effectiveness with sales increases, event attendance, coupon redemption or other numeric measures. Later on you will find out why these metrics, by themselves, do not measure effectiveness.

I will present logical, common-sense arguments that will establish the reality of both the problems and the solutions. If you're a person who thinks that "proof" has to be statistical in nature, you're missing the big picture. If you keep an open mind and understand proof in a broader sense, you're going to love this book.

Part Two - Solutions

The second part of the book contains the disarmingly simple S.T.E.P. that can be taken to fix the existing problems. By providing specific philosophies, ideas and actions, this part will help prepare the industry to carry out its assigned mission, which is to change behavior by changing knowledge, beliefs and attitudes.

This part presents The Fifteen Secrets of Extremely Persuasive Advertising. Included in this section is S.T.E.P (Strategies and Tactics for Effective Persuasion), which contains the criteria which should be used to evaluate advertising.

There are several intriguing ideas here, including a discussion of the limitations of the popular focus group research format and the simple three-step research process which will measure the effectiveness of an ad or ad campaign.

TABLE OF CONTENTS

- Who Needs Training?
- Why Is It Necessary?
- Special Presentations
- Presentation Highlights

PREFACE

This book was started as a college text about creativity. Early on, I identified several serious problems with the industry, specifically in the creative process. Things that nobody else was writing or talking about. This is the industry I love, and I couldn't ignore what I saw.

The result is this book, a sweeping indictment of the advertising industry and a recipe for righting its wrongs. At first, I was embarrassed that it had taken me thirty-five years to see the ad biz for what it has become. Then I remembered that there's no indication anyone else has figured it out yet, so I didn't feel so bad.

This is unlike any other book about advertising you will find on bookstore shelves. In these pages you will find no review, purview or overview. No precious stories about great people in advertising or collections of award-winning ads. No litany of statistics or research findings. No theory about how to run a profitable agency. No clues on how to get a job.

This is an exposé focused on the heart of the industry - creating ads. Advertising is an industry that has some very big problems, but it is too busy to notice. Several major problems are crippling the advertising business, but the industry doesn't admit it or even see it.

I don't have a personal vendetta against advertising or anyone in it. I enjoy the advertising business with all its intricacies and eccentricities. My love of the industry has driven me to write about its problems and how to solve them.

PART I

THE PROBLEMS

Chapter 1

OK, SO HERE'S THE DEAL

The Problem

Most of this book is dedicated to identifying major issues that plague the advertising industry. All these problems work together to cause or reinforce the other problems.

Ad agencies and advertisers have forgotten what advertising should do and how it should do it. Most of the advertising produced in this country has substantial flaws that severely limit its value as a business communication tool. The result is ineffective advertising that gives nothing to the potential consumer and the advertiser.

Impotent ads make it look like the mass media are incapable of doing the job advertisers have asked them to do for decades, which is to deliver information people want and need to make intelligent purchase decisions.

In panic mode, advertisers have lost faith in the mass media, and are turning to the Internet, product placement in TV and movies, cell phones and promotions to try to excite their audiences.

The problem isn't with the media, it's with the quality and content of the ads created by ad agencies and advertisers.

It doesn't make any difference which media advertisers choose to use; as long as ads and messages contain little or nothing for the consumer, advertisers will continue to waste billions of ad dollars every year because people will not pay attention to advertising that doesn't give them what they need and want.

Most of the advertising being done deprives buyers of the valuable information advertising was designed to deliver, and does not help people make smart purchasing decisions.

The Peril

The peril to which I refer is that continued production of misguided, ineffective ads will ultimately make advertising useless to a large number of both advertisers and their target audiences. When large numbers of companies reach the point of conviction or concern about ineffective ads that waste huge amounts of money and resources, mass media advertising will cease to be a viable marketing tool. At this point, the ad industry will shrink dramatically and become a shadow of its former self.

Nobody Cares

There is a great deal of interest in certain key industries in our economy – housing, automotive, airlines, high tech, agriculture, education and finance. Advertising, the most visible industry doesn't get much attention other than at Super Bowl time. We worry when housing starts are down, but not that well over half of all advertising produced is worthless.

Perhaps the lack of concern about the advertising business is caused by people's unhappiness with advertising. Consumers would rather not be assaulted with it, that's for sure. The people who pay for the advertising aren't all that pleased either.

Some advertisers don't think their advertising is working. Some think it could and should be doing more to increase sales. Others don't know whether or not it's working.

Most advertisers are frustrated because advertising is subject to the Goldilocks Syndrome— it's hard to know if you're doing too much, too little, or about the right amount of advertising.

You Want Problems? I Got Your Problems

The business community should be concerned about the advertising industry because it affects just about everyone in some way. It's easy to conclude that advertising isn't meeting the needs of either the general public or the advertisers. Al and Laura Ries put it beautifully in *The Fall of Advertising & The Rise of PR* when they wrote, "...advertising is art. It has lost its communication function."

The inability of the advertising industry to satisfy either consumers or advertisers is due to ten related internal problems. These ten problems work together to cause one overarching problem: Advertisers and their agencies frequently produce ineffective advertising. The "they" here refers to both advertisers and their ad agencies.

1. They have forgotten why advertising exists.
2. They don't know the difference between clever and creative.
3. The players have conflicting approaches and agendas.
4. They aren't giving their audience what they want.
5. There is no definition of great.
6. They're not using research correctly.
7. They're producing "onezies," not campaigns.
8. The approval process is meaningless.
9. The award show is advertising's drug of choice.
10. They don't train their people.

5

Biiiiiig Problems

The industry's problems involve widespread attitudes, beliefs and ways of doing business. The combined result of these factors is ineffective advertising that is a monstrous waste of advertisers' money. If the fashion industry were as off-base as the advertising industry, we would all be wearing large plastic leaf bags.

When you take a critical look at today's advertising, you'll see a lot of advertisers and agencies that don't know what to expect from advertising or how to create persuasive ads.

I'm not saying that all advertising is bad. A lot of effective advertising is being done by gifted and intelligent people. My concern is that a majority of advertising, when measured by effectiveness criteria, is ill-conceived, ineffective, and a waste of time, effort and money.

Too Busy to Notice

How can so many big problems in such a visible industry go unnoticed? It's a high-energy, high-tension business. You're charging so fast to get to the next deadline, meeting or new business pitch, you don't have time to consider the fundamental underpinnings of the business.

When you're waist deep in the advertising muck, you don't see the big-picture poisons that have contaminated the ad biz.

When you're learning the business, you take as truth what is said and commonly believed. Only when you stop accepting the status quo and take time to ask some tough questions does advertising's desperate situation become obvious. The number, seriousness and pervasiveness of the problems are disturbing.

The Industry Sees Problems

Articles and books voice concerns about the state of the industry. People should be concerned. For one thing, employment in ad agencies is shrinking. According to the Labor Department, industry employment has decreased from 496,500 in 2000 to 424,900 in 2004, a decrease of over fourteen percent.

Also, ad spending is not growing as fast as it did during the 1990s, a time when advertising was a hot commodity. Mind you, it is still growing.

New Media

Frequently we hear concerns about advertisers moving money, which used to automatically go into standard advertising channels, into the Internet and other non-traditional vehicles. This is nothing more than the normal changes you see when technology changes.

We heard this when television invaded radio's domain. We heard it again when cable TV fragmented the heretofore monolithic audience. Satellite radio and iPods have traditional radio stations scrambling for listeners. TiVo, DVR, and other products enable TV viewers to avoid commercials completely.

The Internet and round-the-clock cable TV news are making it even harder for newspapers to retain their readers or to attract the younger generations to whom newspapers are of little interest.

Advertisers and ad agencies that want to be competitive are adjusting to the new media. They are learning about the opportunities and problems these newcomers bring to the industry.

People will find ways to handle whatever problems there are. They always do. The opportunities are exciting, and will force advertisers and marketers to develop strategies and programs that are more targeted, more effective and more efficient than those we have now.

There are problems in the ad industry, but there are always problems in all businesses. That's life. The advertising industry sees problems that are normal and expected, and not all that serious.

The Industry Doesn't See the Serious Problems

Even when advertising industry problems are discussed, you will see almost nothing in the media about the ten problems discussed in this book. That's unfortunate, because these fundamental problems threaten the advertising industry's future viability. It seems like nobody is terribly happy with advertising.

Consumers

The average person doesn't like and doesn't want to be exposed to advertising because it interrupts their entertainment. They think there is too much of it, and that it is annoying. When most people don't like your product, try to avoid it and wish it would go away, you have a problem.

Advertisers

Advertisers feel advertising is expensive, inefficient and ineffective. They don't think they are getting their money's worth, and many are looking for more effective forms of communication than the traditional mass media of radio, TV, newspapers, magazines and outdoor.

Ad Agencies

Agencies are under increasing pressure from clients to prove that their advertising is effective. In spite of increasing pressure for advertising accountability, nobody has come up with a satisfactory way of measuring advertising effectiveness, which has left advertisers and agencies feeling very frustrated.

A lot of people think that sales is how you measure effectiveness. It is not. This will be explained in Chapter 5.

Product Defined

For convenience, I use the word "product" in a broad sense, to include products, services, solutions and concepts. Product means whatever is being advertised, not just a physical product.

Chapter 2

PROBLEM #1: THEY HAVE FORGOTTEN WHY ADVERTISING EXISTS

Advertising's Job Defined

Ever since the Romans started putting advertising on buildings, the job of advertising has been to deliver information that encourages people to take an action. Town criers were another early form of advertising, strolling the streets while shouting out public service announcements and information about the products and services in nearby shops. The next time you're irritated about how advertising gets in the way of the fun stuff, remember that there was no way to turn off or mute the town criers.

The vehicles used to deliver advertising have changed, but the job of advertising has not. Advertising has a specific job in the marketing mix: to change knowledge, beliefs and attitudes; to help move people toward the point where they change their minds and purchasing habits.

Ask advertisers and ad agency people to define the job of advertising, and you will get a variety of answers. Increase sales. Inform. Generate name awareness. Foster good will. Entertain. Win awards.

These are all part of the landscape, but the only real job of advertising is the same as it was when ads started with "hear ye, hear ye." By changing knowledge, beliefs and attitudes, advertising should help persuade people to take a desired action. That's advertising's job – nothing more, nothing less.

Leo Burnett, quoted in *100 LEO's*, said "Advertising says to people, 'Here's what we've got. Here's what it will do for you. Here's how to get it.'"

11

Another advertising legend, William Bernbach, quoted in *Bill Bernbach*, once said, "Our job is to sell our clients' merchandise...not ourselves. Our job is to kill the cleverness that makes us shine instead of the product. Our job is to simplify, to tear away the unrelated, to pluck out the weeds that are smothering the product message."

Don't Underestimate Advertising's Possibilities

Asking advertising to do anything less than assist in the persuasion process, such as settling for name familiarity, shows lack of faith in the advertising concept and in the ability of people to create powerful advertising.

A lot of advertising today just gives the company or product name and makes a quick statement about how their product is better than the competition. The statement is usually brief and bland, and there is seldom any support for the claim. Not exactly the kind of stuff that will get people to change their minds and habits.

They Don't Appreciate How Tough It Is to Persuade

Advertisers and agencies have one huge blind spot. They greatly underestimate the difficulty of changing a person's mind. As a result, they don't take the job of persuasion seriously enough and don't create ads that are capable of doing this difficult job.

Here's why it is so tough to persuade people via advertising:

- Nobody wants to be exposed to advertising.
- Everybody is skeptical of what advertising says.
- A lot of people change TV channels and radio

stations when ads come on. They also rush by print ads.

- Very few people remember any advertising to which they are exposed. Most can't even name the advertiser.

- Even when they enjoy a commercial, people usually don't remember the message or the name of the advertiser.

- The average outdoor board viewing time is two seconds.

- Virtually all Internet ads carry a "skip this ad" or "close" icon.

Advertisers should not take this task lightly. Crafting advertising that does what it is supposed to do is a formidable task. When you underestimate the size of the hurdle, you don't jump as high.

When you don't think it's all that tough to persuade someone to use your product, you don't hold your advertising to as high a standard. You don't require it to be as strong, to communicate as clearly, to be as memorable.

Why Is It So Hard to Persuade?

Take yourself as an example. You have habits, developed over the years, which largely determine your actions during your waking hours. What you eat, what you do for fun, how you dress, what music you listen to, the kind of movies you see, what you do on vacation, and what you look for in a date or spouse.

Your habits were formed in one of two ways. Either you tried a number of alternatives and found that one works best for you, or you have always done it this way and it works well enough that you don't see the need of trying another way.

In either case, you do what you do because you are convinced it is best for you. You have to make thousands of these decisions during your lifetime, and you don't like to change your habits unless you are convinced an alternative may have more to offer.

Along Comes Advertising

Advertising's aims to convince you that you are uninformed, misinformed, misguided, underachieving, out of style or downright wrong.

If you want to be socially, fashionably, intellectually, culinarily, athletically, domestically, sexually or culturally correct, you need to buy a certain product.

Not an easy task, considering the high volume of ads a person is exposed to every day, and that people are generally very skeptical of any claim in the mass media. The industry does a good job of self-policing for honesty and transparency, but that doesn't make any difference to the general public.

So What Are We Doing?

The job of advertising is clear. Common sense would tell you that advertisers and their ad agencies should be creating advertising that seeks to persuade, to change minds. But much of the advertising we view, hear and read is designed with the primary objective of entertaining.

When you watch TV, see how many commercials follow a common formula. The first twenty or so seconds are taken up with a semi-humorous exposition of the problem or a competitor's product.

This is followed by a few seconds about the advertiser's product. Often it's little more than telling people to use the advertiser's product as the better alternative.

Is this the kind of advertising Leo Burnett and Bill Bernbach envisioned? Of course not. It's advertainment, not advertising. It makes no Big Promise, and gives the viewer no reasons to believe the claim being made.

Leaf through a couple of the magazines you have around your house or office. Isn't it interesting how many of the full-page and two-page ads have only a few words, what we call short copy? In the ad biz, it's chic to do short headlines and short copy. It makes for a clean, simple, nice looking ad. Some ads aspire to being art.

Is this effective advertising? It can be for some products in the right circumstances. However, this format usually doesn't give enough practical or emotional information, and in most cases won't be strong enough to change minds.

Do not underestimate the customer's desire for information in advertising. It you do, you will waste time, money and opportunity on advertising that never has a chance of doing its assigned task. **Advertising is business communication. It's not art and it's not entertainment.**

Chapter 3

PROBLEM #2: THEY DON'T KNOW THE DIFFERENCE BETWEEN CLEVER AND CREATIVE

When discussing advertising, most people use the words clever and creative to denote the same thing. They are not the same thing. The difference between clever and creative is not generally understood, even by advertising professionals, but there is a major difference between the two.

This Is Clever

Most advertising agencies and advertisers think they are doing creative advertising, good advertising. The majority think it is persuasive, but a lot of it is not.

In some cases they are doing clever, cute, entertaining advertising which has some momentary interest. People who are clever may also be creative if they create something. Clever advertising often is mildly entertaining. It generates ooohs, aaahs and kudos, but is usually not powerful enough to persuade.

I once heard a man comment on a TV spot, "The ad was good, but I don't know how good the product is." That is the problem with clever advertising. It wants to entertain rather than persuade.

The agency loves it because it looks good and could win awards. The client loves it because it looks good and gets good comments and chuckles around the office. At best, the public may find it mildly entertaining, but of no lasting interest and leaving no lasting impression.

In other cases people are doing advertising that is unimaginative, dull, boring, and utterly devoid of information or interest. Clever advertising can also be creative, but advertising with no information or interest has virtually no chance of being creative.

This Is Creative

To be creative, you have to create something. Artists are creative when they finish a painting or sculpture. Advertising people are not creative when they finish an ad. Why not, you ask? Because their job is to create results, not just an ad.

The ad is a tool, a means to the end, such as sales, dissemination of new product information or coupon distribution. They have made an ad, but haven't created anything until they get results.

Advertising should create changes in knowledge, beliefs and attitudes, making it more likely that a person will take a desired action. Advertising that doesn't set the stage for improved results for a client is not creative. Perhaps clever or entertaining, but not creative. There is truth in the old advertising adage, "It's not creative unless it sells."

Tougher Than You Think

Coming up with truly creative advertising is more difficult because we see so much advertising that is only clever. We find it tempting to take the easy path and mimic a clever approach, rather than worry about doing the harder and less entertaining job of changing minds.

Also, the advertising award show books, *Communication Arts* magazine and the like don't indicate which ads were effective in changing knowledge, beliefs and attitudes, in addition to being clever and award-winning.

Creative people looking for something to inspire an idea have no clue whether an ad was powerful enough to create actions and results, or merely clever. They often have never been taught that advertising is supposed to change minds, that it is extremely difficult to do so, and that there are some things that make ads more likely to be persuasive.

Being Creative Rocks!

People who are creative produce something valuable. A lot of "creatives" (art directors, copywriters and creative directors) are clever. They are interesting, even fascinating at times. They are fun to be with because they take a looser and more amusing look at life and their world.

The outstanding ones are those who produce advertising that has a higher probability of getting people to think differently about a product. Call it effective advertising or good advertising or creative advertising. They should all should mean the same thing to you. Only the people who produce it deserve to be called experts in their field.

Reserve the adjective "creative" for those people who make a Big Promise to their audience, then give them reasons to believe it. They work hard to answer The Question, the one question every customer asks, and every ad should answer. "Why should I buy this product, from you, now?"

Why Have We Given Up Trying to Be Effective?

Every year, America's advertisers and ad agencies waste billions of dollars because they settle for advertising that is clever but not creative. The high percentage of ads I would classify as advertainment indicates that a lot of advertising practitioners don't comprehend the role of advertising in the persuasion process.

Sometimes they don't believe in the power of advertising. Often they don't know how to produce advertising that has the strength required to change minds. At times, they have been seduced by the excitement of being part of the entertainment business.

What's Up with Advertising?

To understand why I'm so concerned with advertainment, let's take a look at what advertising is supposed to do. I like the way advertising legend Fairfax Cone put it. "Advertising is what you do when you can't go see somebody. That's all it is."

Nobody would argue that face-to-face conversation is generally the most effective method of communication. The farther you get from the person, the harder it is to get your point across.

If you were standing face to face with someone and had one minute to try to convince them to give you $100, would you tell them jokes or would you tell them how they benefited from giving you the money? A lot of advertising is settling for telling jokes.

Ohh, Dairy Queen, What Were You Thinking?

I have been seeing an excellent example of this joke telling problem on TV recently. The advertiser is Dairy Queen, a major favorite with me. You can't beat their ice cream and their advertising is usually good, which makes this commercial stand out.

The commercial begins with a pregnant woman and her husband at an amusement park. He daydreams a nice little scene, then she daydreams about him having a baby and yelling at her, "You did this to me." This takes most of the commercial. The commercial ends with a brief show of delicious

DQ products and some forgettable copy about eating their products being like a dream.

There are two serious problems with this commercial. First, showing a man in the throes of childbirth and screaming at his wife then cutting to the DQ products borders on disgusting. Second, the main job of food advertising should be to make the viewer hungry. Why spend most of commercial trying to be funny, when you have such delicious looking and tasting products?

Something to Take Pride In?

The desire to be funny shows up in print ads as well. One that caught my attention was a full color magazine ad done by United Healthcare Insurance Company. The photo, which took up the entire page, was taken in a grassy area which looks like it could be in Africa. It had a quality appearance.

Four lions are shown on the far right side, staring intently at a man on the left side of the ad who is wearing a man-made lion head. In back of him is a sound man holding his boom mike. There are a couple of lines of copy based on the concept of common sense, and there's a logo in the lower right side of the ad.

The photo concept is definitely sophisticated humor, and the logo stands out. The problem is that the ad doesn't give any reasons to believe the Big Promise, which I assume is that choosing this insurance company is just a matter of common sense. Clever and humorous, for sure. Capable of changing a reader's mind about their insurance coverage? Highly doubtful.

Entertaining vs. Effective Advertising

We are pummeled daily with so much advertainment, it's easy to accept that as the "right" way to do advertising. To obviate the difference between advertainment and effectiveness-based advertising, here is what these two approaches might look like in the same advertising situation.

The entertaining approach is shown on the next page, followed by a more effective type of ad.

Advertainment Television Commercial

Hip Music Throughout

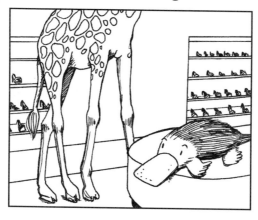

"If you have feet, we have your shoes at Ed's Shoes."

Effectiveness-Based Television Commercial

"At Ed's Shoes, we stock over 4,000 pairs of shoes at all times. And they're discount priced."

"At Ed's Shoes, you will find your size and width in a style you like or we'll give you $25 off your next pair. "

"If you have feet, we have your shoes at Ed's Shoes."

Chapter 4

PROBLEM #3: THE PLAYERS HAVE CONFLICTING APPROACHES AND AGENDAS

The advertising industry is populated by a wide variety of intelligent, talented people. There's plenty of independence and ego to go around, and widely differing approaches to advertising. It would be safe to say that everyone is not on the same page of the hymnal. In fact, there are substantial personal and professional differences among the people involved.

To fully comprehend the difficulty of changing from a clever advertising philosophy to a creative one, you have to understand how the various players in this game think.

The Client

The client is comprised of as many as three types of people. First: the person who handles the day-to-day work. This person works closely with the account executive from the agency. In smaller companies, it can be the marketing person or even the owner. In larger firms, it's the ad manager.

Second: in medium to large organizations, the day-to-day client contact may report to the second type of person, usually called a marketing manager, marketing director or even vice president of marketing.

Third: top management, the person or people who don't have much, if anything, to do with advertising until it's time for a final blessing and approval of it before it hits the media.

Everyone on the client side wants the same thing: results. Though they are happy when their agency wins awards, they expect a return on their advertising investment, usually using sales as the measure. If the results aren't there, out come the research numbers to prove they did due diligence and followed the path the data told them to take.

This is usually enough to ensure nobody in-house gets fired, though the agency is always a handy scapegoat no matter what the research shows.

The Creative Team

A creative team consists of a copywriter, an art director, and a creative director to whom they report. These are the most important people in the advertising business because they actually create the ads.

Creatives relish their freedom, and demand minimal rules and boundaries on the creative process. The creative team also wants to have control of the creative product, though they realize that they have to share control with the client, who has the ultimate power to accept or reject their creative work.

Where Creatives Find Happiness

Creatives love to create things. Copywriters delight in finding just the right word, in setting the proper tone. Art Directors strive to put all the pieces together in a powerful and appealing visualization. The process of creating is a reward in itself. They also enjoy the recognition of their peers in creative competitions.

Clients and account handlers often have little understanding or appreciation of the creative mind and the creative product. The creative team appreciates the "atta boy" and "great job" comments from the agency account executives and the client, and creative awards are visible proof of the excellence in their field.

It's Fun, But It's Not Easy

Creatives are the heart of the agency, but theirs is not always an easy or rewarding job. They have to make sense of the sometimes confusing or unclear direction given them by the client and account manager, and changes of direction which may unexpectedly occur at any time during the creative process.

They rack their brains to come up with just the right concept, copy and visuals, only to have the account managers and the client ask questions about little details like the color of the woman's skirt or whether the door should be totally shut or ajar just a crack.

Clients frequently suggest changes in visual or copy, in sometimes misguided efforts to improve the product that the creative team has painstakingly crafted. Can you blame creatives for thinking clients get in the way of great advertising?

Who Gets to Present Creative?

Some agencies have their creative team, or at least the creative director, present their work directly to the client. That makes sense. They worked long and hard on it, and know it better than anyone else. The downside of this approach is that creatives can get feisty and dismissive in defense of their work, which can lead to tense exchanges and an unhappy client.

Other agencies have the account managers present the creative without the creative team being present. I have done this a lot, and though it is commonly done, it's not the answer. Even seasoned account managers don't know all the detailed thinking behind the work, so they can neither explain it nor answer questions about it like the creative team.

Still other agencies make a practice of having both the creative team and the account management team present together. This allows a more thorough and intelligent discussion, more accurate communication, and a more harmonious relationship among everyone. This is definitely the way to go.

The Beleaguered Account Manager

As tough as the creatives have it, account service people are in the toughest position – the middle. Called "suits" by the creative types, these poor souls play director, messenger, arbiter and translator as they shuffle back and forth between the creative team and the client, trying to make everyone happy while getting the work created, approved and produced on time and on budget.

Creatives may not respect suits, or at least not the younger ones, but being a suit is an extremely demanding job. It is not for the faint of heart. It takes a wide variety of skills and a huge storehouse of knowledge to be successful. When account executives call on their first client, they are expected to have a working knowledge in a daunting number of areas:

Print production	Hot agencies
TV production	Current ad trends
Radio production	The Internet
Outdoor ad production	Accounting & billing
Media planning	Media buying
The creative process	The client and industry

Colors	Research techniques
Grammar and spelling	Direct response
Public relations	Promotions

The account executive is a generalist, facilitator, organizer and synthesizer, relying on specialists to provide information, ideas and assistance. With all that account executives have to know and learn, they rely on creative people to tell them what good creative is, and on agency management to define their relationship with creatives.

Account managers get information and objectives from the client, write up the creative brief and answer questions for the creative team. Account managers, especially younger ones, usually have little to say about what is produced by their creatives.

Even if the account manager disagrees with the creative team's output, the account manager's job is to present it to the client. The prevailing feeling among creatives is that the account executive's job is not just to present, but also to promote and defend their work if the creatives aren't present.

Account managers' objectives are simple. Don't drop any of the balls they are juggling. Maintain cordial relationships with the creatives. Keep the clients happy. Don't make waves.

Creatives Look Down on Account Managers

In the opinion of creatives, account service people are substantially less important than the creatives. Whatever the title, to creatives, they are a suit. Lest you misconstrue the true meaning of this term, it does not refer to manner of dress. It is a term of derision, and the complete moniker is "empty suit."

It reflects the creatives' perception that a suit is a superficial jack-of-all-trades who knows a little bit about a lot of subjects, creativity not being one of them.

Who Wants What

By now, you will recognize that the players have different agendas and different perspectives. Advertisers want results and ads that have tested well so nobody can blame them for disappointing results.

Ad agency account managers want to make clients happy and avoid confrontations with clients and creatives. Creatives want to do powerful communication and be respected and recognized for it.

Not exactly a formula for harmony and agreement. Rather, a recipe for confusion, underachievement and money ill spent.

The Teeter Totter Is Not Teetering

There's another way of looking at the people involved in advertising. Let's put the account service people and the client people together into the one category--"suits". They are all managers, so they share a lot of attitudes and practices. Their approach to advertising tends to be more practical and businesslike than the creative types, who are the second category.

These two groups represent the two personalities of advertising. One is a buttoned-down, nose-to-the-grindstone type. The other is wild and crazy and fun-loving. In a perfect world, the two personalities would work in harmony to produce an intelligent and artistic product.

It is apparent from looking at the advertising being done that the creative side is firmly in control of the advertising business right now. There is quite a bit of advertainment, a lot of humor and cleverness, but not much persuasion.

It's like the big kid who controls the movement of the teeter totter. The wacky creative guy is sitting on the ground, making faces at the staid business guy helplessly dangling in the air. This isn't good, because nothing productive is happening. Only one person is contributing to a game meant for two.

Different people have different agendas and driving forces behind what they do. The players don't share the same set of evaluative criteria, so they look at advertising with different eyes, different expectations and different definitions of "good". In any business, that's a real problem. In advertising, it's preventing the teeter totter from teetering. And tottering.

We have to get the teeter totter teetering again. We need to provide the business side of the business with the tools to make advertising more effective.

But how? Somebody has to stand up and say that the emperor has no clothes. Somebody has to remind the advertising industry that the purpose is to change minds and habits, not make people laugh. Sure, it feels good to entertain as a way to make your point, but all entertainment and no "sales pitch" is simply not doing the job for most advertisers.

You have to give people who plan, create, present and approve advertising an understanding of what makes advertising effective, that is, persuasive. Not entertaining, but mind changing. Advertising must answer the consumer's question, "Why should I buy this product, from you, now?"

Chapter 5

PROBLEM #4: THEY AREN'T GIVING THEIR AUDIENCE WHAT THEY WANT

Good marketing is built on a simple premise: find out what people want and need, and give it to them. Any successful company knows that if you want to be a success, you absolutely must give your customers what they want or need.

So why do so few advertisers tell people about the main benefit of their products? Why do so many spend their money to entertain rather than promote the product?

Having removed from their advertising most of the helpful information, both emotional and factual, these advertisers and their agencies have once again escaped the awful prospect of having to come to grips with one of the most frightening things in marketing-defining their "Big Promise."

The Question

"Why should I buy this product, from you, now?" This is the three-part question that potential customers ask themselves all the time, usually without realizing it.

It should form the basis for all marketing activities, but consistently stumps both clients and agencies. Advertisers have to have a good answer if they want a shot at the sale. If advertisers don't have a clear, concise idea of the value of their product to the customer, how can they expect their customers to have one?

The importance of answering The Question is obvious. You would assume every advertiser has a good answer for it. Nope. A lot of intelligent, successful ad managers, marketing directors, and owners are unable to give a succinct answer to this critical question. In many cases, it is because theirs is an undifferentiated product.

When asked, "Why should people buy this product, from you, now?" a common answer is something like, "Our product is pretty much as good as any of our competitors." Another popular response involves a listing of features and benefits that would put the most ardent consumer to sleep.

Other answers are built around vague generalizations relating to superior customer service, higher quality, greater reliability, better engineering and other equally vague promises.

An ad agency should not spend a second on concept or write a word of copy until the client has provided a concise, specific answer to The Question. Agency person, don't let your client off the hook on this. Threaten to withhold free lunches until you get your answer. That should do the job.

Big Promise Defined

A Big Promise is the most important thing an ad can tell customers. It is the biggest personal benefit the product offers them. A Big Promise is the answer to The Question. It's useful to attract new customers as well as remind current customers of the wisdom of their decision.

A Big Promise is not a product description. It should be no longer than a few words. It should be as specific as possible. It doesn't even have to be a complete sentence. For any product, there are several ways of expressing the Big Promise. Here are a few product category examples. Big Promises for individual companies and products must be much more specific, and be easily related to that company or product.

Product	Possible Big Promises
Sports car	Freedom, manliness, power, excitement
"Name" apparel	Belonging, status, hipness
Free checking	Money, power, importance
Posh hair salon	Status, superiority, sex appeal
Sporting event	Family time, fun, identify with a winner

Identifying a Big Promise doesn't seem too difficult, but you would be amazed at how many advertisers can't give you a simple answer when asked to identify the single most important thing their product offers their customers. They drone on and on, describing their product in laborious detail, but never really answer the question.

They Give No Reason to Believe the Big Promise

The Big Promise is necessary, but it isn't enough by itself. When you make a promise, you have to give people reasons to believe it. You have to support your contention with specific information. Factual, emotional, or best of all, both.

When someone makes a promise to you, your natural inclination is to wonder if that person can deliver on it. Because we expect a certain amount of puffery from advertising, our natural doubt of ad claims is huge. That is why it is so important not just to make claims, but to back them up.

Don't just claim to make the best widget on the market, detail the specific things that make your widget superior. Is it a key ingredient, process, quality control or the unique design? Give results from comparative tests that clearly show your widget is top dog. Let satisfied customers give powerful testimonials for you.

Even if your product is established and has a great reputation, keep giving support to your Big Promise. New people are entering the market all the time. They need to know. They want to know.

Product, Product, Product

When you see an ad that doesn't have a Big Promise and/or support for it, the problem may be more than just shoddy creative work. In many cases, it may be a product problem.

By far the most important determinant of business success is the product. For maximum success, the product should offer something the competition doesn't. Products which have a point of difference and an indication of superiority make it so much easier to do effective advertising.

Most products or services have direct competitors, usually quite a few. With the proliferation of undifferentiated me-too products, a large number of advertisers and their ad agencies have given up trying to provide demonstrable evidence of product superiority because they don't think it exists.

One of the underlying problems is that many clients, perhaps even most, can't give a single persuasive reason why their product is better than competitors' offerings. They may give you little facts, perceptions and beliefs, but few will be able to come up with a simple, strong statement of difference and superiority.

The Milk Story

One good example of the inability to come to grips with a serious product problem--call it the head-in-the-sand syndrome—is the "Got Milk?" national ad campaign.

What is their creative approach and their big
creative idea? Show celebrities, athletes and other
well-known people with a milk mustache, along with
the "Got Milk?" headline and a few words in small
type talking about the weight loss or calcium benefits
of milk.

I think the milk mustache is a very small
idea. Lest you think the milk mustache is a stroke
of genius, every agency that has ever worked
on a milk campaign has thought of using the
milk mustache.

Most of them realized that it doesn't make people
want milk, doesn't make an obvious Big Promise,
and doesn't reinforce or symbolize the message
or product benefits. Most agencies have had the
good taste to say, "That's stupid" and look for ideas
with substance.

The only thing different about this mustache
campaign is that it slaps them on celebrities. The main
reason people think this campaign is good is that it
uses celebrities. For some reason, people like to see
pictures of famous people. I'll leave the explanation
for this phenomenon to the psychiatrists. Can they
really believe that people will drink milk because
Doctor Phil has a milk mustache? Come on.

The client here is a great group of intelligent,
honest, nice, hard working, well-meaning dairy
farmers and others in the industry. Their agency
is large and highly respected. The campaign is
familiar to a large percentage of the population. So
what's the problem?

First of all, shame on the client for not realizing
or acknowledging that advertising cannot increase
per capita consumption of white milk. For many
years, per capita consumption of milk has been
declining. It has continued to decline in spite of
the money spent on this famous ad campaign.

Advertising Age magazine reported that the mustache campaign began in 1996 on a $110 million budget. In 1998, it was up to $190 million. Beverage Marketing Corporation shows that the 2002 budget was $110 million. Assuming the yearly expenditure for the intervening years was $100 million, the total mustache campaign cost for its first seven years was about $750 million.

According to Beverage Marketing Corporation, per capita consumption of milk between 1995 and 2002 declined by up to two percent every year except 1996, when it increased by three-tenths of one percent.

In spite of the expenditure of around three quarters of a billion dollars on the national mustache campaign, milk consumption continued its decline to record lows.

Now comes the part that blows me away. The report goes on to say, "BMC continues to believe that fluid milk per capita consumption declines and volumetric trends would have been greater without the effect of the national generic fluid milk advertising and promotional programs." In plain English, consumption would have been lower if the campaign had not been done.

This is nothing more than unfounded speculation. The fact is, no one can know what would have happened in the absence of advertising.

If you spent three quarters of a billion dollars over seven years and sales kept declining, and someone said, "Well, it could have been worse," would you sit back and say, "Golly, you may be right. I think I'll pour some more money down that hole."

One of the reasons for declining milk consumption is concern over some of its contents, including calories, carbs, cholesterol and growth hormones. A bigger reason is that there are a lot more alternative beverages out there than there used to be.

Their easy availability has certainly hurt milk consumption. Bottled water, flavored waters, juices, regular and diet sodas, energy drinks, coffee, and coffee drinks are heavily promoted. Kids see them all the time on television and billboards, looking fun, hip and exciting.

Another big reason is that milk is not perceived as an adult drink. It's for kids, to be consumed for its nutritional qualities, not its taste. "Drink your milk" grates on kids, and they want very much to be able to drink something else.

Time-starved families eat out at fast food places quite a bit, where parents are more likely to let kids have soda pop as a treat, rather than force milk on them. Kids see milk as a symbol of parental control, and this tantalizing taste of adulthood and freedom gives the kids even more desire for any of the forbidden elixirs that aren't milk.

For kids in high school and beyond, milk drinking isn't even an option unless they are athletes. From then on, it's all about looking like an adult, and consuming caffeine in any form-coffee, coffee drinks, soda pop and energy drinks. As if kids need more energy.

For the most part, adults get their milk on cereal, in cheese, yogurt, coffee, coffee drinks and ice cream. Because of their need for calcium to prevent osteoporosis, women of all ages are more likely to drink milk throughout their life. After all, milk is the natural and effective way of getting calcium.

The milk mustache campaign always has a nutritional message in addition to the mustachioed celebrity, and the major reason to drink milk always has been its nutritional value. This is where there is a disconnect between the dairy industry and the consuming public.

The general public uses taste and occasion appropriateness as their two primary evaluative criteria when selecting a drink. For most people, milk's taste is not a strong point. Neither is the fact that it has fat, cholesterol and carbs.

I don't know if the agency has tried to dissuade the milk people from wasting their hard-earned money on a national milk campaign. If they did and the client wouldn't listen, I salute the agency for their noble attempt. Shame on the client for not listening to wise counsel.

However, if the agency was so blinded by the size of the budget that it didn't say anything, or if it just doesn't understand the obvious societal factors which argue against consumption of white milk, shame on it.

In any case, milk industry, I love you folks and it pains me terribly to see what you're doing. This is a product that reached its maximum sales potential quite some time ago, and there's nothing to indicate it will make a comeback.

My advice to you is to stop the ad campaign and use that money to fund development of new products such as flavored milks, flavors to be put into milk at home, and new products that include large amounts of milk, like lattés.

Just think of how much lower milk consumption would be if the latté hadn't come along. The dairy industry owes Starbucks a real debt of gratitude.

How "Got Milk?" Got Started

Here's a little history you might find interesting. The "Got Milk?" campaign began in California as the tag line for a campaign designed to remind people of some situations in which white milk is just what the doctor ordered.

Chocolate cake, cookies, peanut butter and jelly sandwiches, that kind of thing. That's smart. The objective of food advertising should be to make people hungry or thirsty. That campaign did that. Way to go, California milk folks and your agency.

The national group must have liked the line so much that they took it for use in the national campaign. Unfortunately, they don't have a meaningful message like California did.

No Reasons to Believe the Big Promise.

Even when advertisers make a Big Promise and express it with a creative Big Idea, they often don't provide the details and specifics that will seal the deal. It's important to make a promise, but it's not enough. You must give your audience specific information which will allow them to believe your promise.

An alarming number of ads in major national media don't include support for the Big Promise. The amount of information required to support a Big Promise depends on the product. Sometimes, a small amount of copy is all that's needed.

Copy Is Usually Better When it's Longer

If you have been in advertising for any length of time, you have probably heard the old adage that long copy sells more than short copy. That doesn't mean short copy is necessarily an indication of ineffective advertising.

It means that, in situations where factual information is important to the purchasing decision, not giving people facts and information usually results in ineffective advertising. Examples would include mutual funds, most cars, homes, equipment and machinery.

When products are purchased entirely or largely on the basis of emotion, copy is not nearly as important as the emotional feel of the ad, so all-emotion advertising for certain brands and categories makes perfect sense. This includes designer clothing, perfume, expensive watches and jewelry.

Some say that the impact of long copy applies to direct-response advertising, but not to mass media advertising. Wrong. The value of longer copy applies to any medium in situations when people want and need information to help them make a smart decision.

Infomercials Prove the Value of Information

There are a lot of infomercials on TV these days. The growth of cable TV channels has provided a lot of time slots to fill. Infomercials have filled quite a few of them.

We laugh at infomercials because some of them are over the top in terms of acting and forced excitement, but dismissing them as the lunatic fringe of advertising is a mistake. Infomercials are the TV equivalent of long copy print ads. We see an increasing number of them because they work. There certainly is some entertainment value to them, but all of it is in support of the Big Promise, which is why they sell product.

They sell not just because they make a powerful Big Promise. They also give so many specific reasons to believe their claim that it's hard to resist. Nobody will mistake them for art, and agency creatives pooh pooh them, but they are effective in ways that standard advertising can't touch.

Advertising's Gurus Love Long Copy

In further support of the claim that long copy is better, here is what some of the most respected ad men in history have said about the subject. I'm including so many that you may think it's an infomercial for long copy, but I want you to take note of two things.

One, these giants of advertising all agree that long copy is more effective in getting results. Two, most of what the advertising industry produces today does not contain long copy.

David Ogilvy
(Ogilvy & Mather)

ADVOCATE OF LONG COPY

"There is a universal belief in lay circles that people won't read long copy. Nothing could be further from the truth."

"Every advertisement should be a complete sales pitch for your product."

"Research shows that readership falls off rapidly up to 50 words of copy, but drops very little between 50 and 500 words."

"Direct response advertisers know that short copy doesn't sell. In split run tests, long copy invariably outsells short copy."

"Only amateurs use short copy."

43

John Caples

(Copywriter and author of books on advertising)

"Ads with lots of facts are effective. And don't be afraid of long copy. If your ad is interesting, people will read all the copy you can give them. If the ad is dull, short copy won't save it."

Dr. Charles Edwards

(Grad School of Retailing, NY University)

"The more facts you tell, the more you sell. An advertisement's chance for success invariably increases as the number of pertinent merchandise facts included in the advertisement increases."

Claude Hopkins

(Advertising guru)

"The motto is, 'The more you tell the more you sell,' and it has never failed to prove out so in any test we know."

Victor O. Schwab

(Author of "How to Write a Good Advertisement)

"The longer your copy can hold the interest of the greatest number of readers, the likelier you are to induce more of them to act."

"To sum up: the longer your copy can hold people, the more of them you will sell; and the more interesting your copy is, the longer you will hold them. If you can keep your reader interested, you'll have a better chance of propelling him to action. If you cannot do that, then too small an amount of copy won't push him far enough along that road anyway."

Jay Conrad Levinson

(Author, Guerrilla Marketing)

"Remember that long copy works better than short copy. Of all the things people dislike about marketing, "lack of information" comes in second. ("Feeling deceived" is first.)

Make Long Short

Long copy is more effective than short copy, but how long is long? The objective of all writing is to use the fewest, most specific, most powerful words that will make your point.

Don't stop writing before you've communicated everything you want. Don't use one word more than is required to do the job.

When I see a Big Promise and several pieces of information that support it delivered in two or three succinct sentences, I'm thrilled. Bravo!

Hot Buyers Want to Know

The objective of advertising is to change minds so that people will change behavior. The most important part of the target audience is what I call Hot Buyers. These are people who are going to choose between competing products in the very near future.

Whereas other listeners, viewers and readers have little or no interest in a product category, hot buyers are usually actively looking for, and willing to listen to, information that would help them make a smart purchase. These people read body copy because they hope and expect to find factual information.

Hot buyers make frequent use of the Internet because of the readily available information and opportunities for comparison shopping of features and prices.

If an advertiser has a desirable product and a competitive advantage, its agency can probably find some pretty strong things to say about it. Things that will get some people to buy the product. What a shame when advertisers and their agencies give hot buyers weak, non-product related advertainment rather than useful information. Everyone loses.

The National Turkey Federation ad on the next page does everything a commodity food ad should. The picture of the popular roll-up makes you hungry, the headline gives a great Big Promise, the subheads give persuasive facts, and the simple recipe makes it easy to take action. It's an ad that has a high chance of success.

MORE PROTEIN, LESS FAT.
NOTHING TOPS TURKEY.

TURKEY
has
8%
MORE
PROTEIN
than
BEEF
or
CHICKEN
and
0%
SATURATED
FAT*

DELICIOUS, VERSATILE, AND PERFECT FOR PEOPLE COUNTING CARBS.

THAI TURKEY ROLL UP

4, 8-inch whole wheat, high-protein tortillas
Peanut sauce, commercial or homemade
1 lb. oven roasted turkey breast, sliced thin
2 oz. red onion, sliced thin

2 oz. lettuce, washed, drained, chilled, shredded
4 tsp. cilantro, washed, drained, chilled

Spread each tortilla with peanut sauce. Layer each with 4 slices of turkey (4 oz.). Evenly sprinkle each with 1 Tbsp. onion, 1 Tbsp. lettuce and 1 tsp. cilantro. Roll up tightly and cut on the diagonal. Serve chilled.

TURKEY
the perfect protein™

FOR MORE GREAT RECIPES VISIT **eatturkey.com**

*Nutri-Facts Update, reviewed by USDA. 3 oz. cooked serving skinless turkey breast, 3 oz. cooked serving skinless chicken breast, 3 oz. top loin steak trimmed of visible fat.

It's Not a Popularity Contest

A common rationale for creating ads with little copy - and vague, useless copy at that - is "Since people don't like advertising, we might as well entertain them because it will make them less mad at us."

This approach is a sign of surrender from advertisers and agencies which have run out of ideas and have no guts. In many instances, advertisers don't even realize they are doing it.

Get Their Attention?

Advertising people will tell you they use humor, special effects and celebrity spokespersons in TV and radio spots to get attention. After all, it's important to get the attention of your audience so they'll listen to your message. Sounds like a rational approach, but before you buy into this idea, consider a couple of things.

Everyone in the industry assumes it is necessary to get attention. I did for years until I actually took some time and thought about it. I applied common sense to the issue and the answer was obvious. We don't have to get attention. **People are already paying attention. We just have to give them a reason to continue paying attention.**

Why waste time trying to get attention if people are already paying attention to the medium? The job is to retain attention while giving people a compelling message.

The Blind Leading the Blind

In print ads, a common approach is to get attention by using "blind headlines." These headlines give no indication of the product, promise, benefits or anything related to the product. The idea is to make you curious to know what is going on so you will read the body copy.

Advertisers who use blind headlines seem to have forgotten two very important advertising truths. First, eighty percent of readers only read the headline and look at the main visual, and go no further. With a blind ad, they have no chance of getting any message from it.

Second, people don't really like advertising. In fact, they wish it would go away. Thus, most people will not make an effort to understand subtle, unclear or confusing advertising.

As with everything else in advertising, there are effective and ineffective ways to do blind-headline ads. They have a chance to be effective when they don't just rely on double entendres or other plays on words. If they make the reader want to find out more, if they contain specifics, they have a shot.

The same can be said for TV advertising that doesn't let you know the sponsor name until the very end of the spot. Why do this? The hope is that you will watch the entire spot to find out.

The reality is that these spots are so caught up in being intriguing and entertaining that they don't contain any helpful information. Even if you can remember the sponsor name, which is doubtful, there is nothing persuasive connected with it. The ad is a total loss.

How can anyone think that people are going to spend their valuable time trying to figure out what a piece of advertising means? This is something they didn't want to see in the first place. It's not going to happen.

Leave Teasing to Strippers

Whether it's a stripteaser or your older brother making fun of your braces, teasing is commonplace in our society. Teasing goes on in advertising as well, in the form of teaser campaigns.

Usually done in print, TV or outdoor boards, a teaser campaign starts out with a visual, words or combination thereof that tells nothing about the product or advertiser. Over time, information is added until a complete ad is unveiled.

You have probably heard the term, "Getting there is half the fun." It was a great slogan used many years ago by Cunard Steamship Company. It's also the concept behind a strip tease and a teaser advertising campaign.

The objective of a teaser campaign is to generate anticipation and a desire to know what it's all about. While we can all understand that getting there is half the fun on a cruise ship or striptease, the analogy falls short when you're talking about an ad campaign. Teaser campaigns are a big waste of money.

The reason is that most people who have a life don't have the time or the interest to get all pumped up waiting for ads. The people who create them have a ball teasing the public, and they consider themselves quite creative. It's too bad they aren't creating effective advertising.

Why Pay to Say Nothing?

Another problem is that the advertiser gets absolutely nothing from the investment in the teaser part of the campaign. No matter how many teaser ads are shown, no matter how much anticipation and interest may eventually be generated, people still don't know a thing about the product, and the advertiser doesn't get a cent of incremental sales.

A very small percentage of people might look forward to seeing the ads, but no matter how much hype has gone before, once the complete ad is presented, it's just another ad. Whatever intrigue and interest has been generated by the initial part of the campaign is quickly forgotten, and it has no residual effect.

Why would you spend your money on advertising that has no message and often no sponsor identification? Even if they wanted to, people couldn't take any action. So what's the purpose?

The Emotionalization of Advertising

Advertising messages come in two forms, factual and emotional. Both are valid, and ads can be a mix of the two or exclusively one or the other. Emotionalization can best be described as the exclusive use of emotional information in advertising.

This seemingly harmless strategy has quietly, insidiously, become the approach of choice for advertisers, with the misguided approval of their clients.

I have no problem with Nike, Coke, Gucci, Hugo Boss, BMW and other well-known category leaders doing all-emotion advertising. For a select few advertisers, this is an excellent strategy. When you're at the top in your category, you can sometimes get away without saying anything about your product. People are predisposed to like it and buy it because they already perceive it to be highly desirable.

Even the leaders, however, will use factual information in their advertising when introducing a new product or major product improvement.

It's Not For Everyone

What disturbs me is the use of this strategy for unremarkable, undifferentiated products which are nowhere near the top of their category. Especially heinous is the use of the all-emotion approach to introduce new products.

I won't insult your intelligence by detailing what is wrong with this. I'll just ask one question. If you become aware of a new product of possible interest to you, would knowing only its name be enough information for you to make an intelligent decision about the product? Of course not.

All Emotion vs. Emotion/Factual Combination

To make sure the terms are clear, I have included two mock ads that exemplify the difference between an ad with only emotional information and an ad with both emotional and factual information.

The same objective applies to both of the following ads: Make fliers more likely to select Modern Air as their favorite airline. The full page, full color ad would run in such broad-appeal magazines as Time, Newsweek and People.

All Emotional Information

"With Modern Air, getting there is more than half the fun."

Emotional and Factual Information

"All airlines used to give you friendly, smiling flight attendants, free snacks and beverages, free pillows and blankets, and plenty of room for your knees. Now, it's just us."

The Dot.Dumb Debacle

The dot.com fiasco is an excellent example of two common problems in the way advertising is created. The first problem is that the dot.coms did not take a marketing approach to their business. They took the old fashioned, but still fashionable, selling approach.

It never hurts to review the difference between marketing and selling. If you have a selling attitude, you take whatever product you have and try to convince customers they need it.

If you have a marketing attitude, you start by finding out what customers need or want. Then you make it and tell the customers how it solves a problem they have.

Many dot.com founders became so enamored with what they could do that they forgot to ask potential customers if they really wanted and were willing to pay for the capabilities.

The second thing that helped bring about the dot.com collapse was the use of huge amounts of venture capital for advertising that lacked a Big Promise. Most of the ads didn't even tell people what the product was and why it was a good buy. Instead, they chose to entertain or settle for name awareness.

Once again, let's put the blame where it belongs. Shame on the advertising agencies that created, produced and billed handsomely for these totally useless commercials. Shame on them for not knowing that they had no chance of success with this strategy.

For a few years, the dot.coms dominated Super Bowl advertising. Now, you may see one a year. What more can I say?

Why Do It?

Companies which shouldn't do all-emotion advertising usually do so for one of two reasons. Either they think it can work for them because it works for the top dogs, or they have given up hope of making any strides against the better-known competition on the basis of product attributes and benefits. In neither case will the results be positive, and much money will be wasted.

A large part of the advertising industry has given up trying to give out any sort of factual information, settling for emotional information only. They ask only that their advertising establish name awareness and a "feel", a personality for the company or product.

A lot of advertisers who really would like to do all-emotion ads feel guilty about that approach, so they pay lip service to promoting their product. Their ads are part humor and part standard product promotion, and end up being neither fish nor fowl. They don't have enough time to be either funny or informational. These ads are neither funny nor persuasive.

Chapter 6

PROBLEM #5: THEY KNOW WHAT THEY LIKE. THEY DON'T KNOW WHAT'S GOOD.

What Makes a Good Advertising Agency?

When you use the services of an advertising agency, how do you know if they have done a good job for you? Here are some of the most common answers:

- Our agency has won creative awards for its work.
- They do very hip, funny stuff.
- Our sales are up.
- They do good work, and they charge a fair price.
- They provide excellent service in a lot of areas.
- They are smart and know a lot about advertising.
- They meet deadlines.
- People talk about our ads.
- Our ads test well with focus groups.

All these answers are wrong because they do not measure the things for which advertising is primarily responsible – <u>changes</u> in knowledge, beliefs and attitudes, ultimately leading to changes in behavior.

Forget Purchase Intent

You may have noticed that "purchase intent" is not included in the key factors. Many companies look closely at this, but I prefer to stick with the big three factors for two reasons.

57

First, people will often tell you they intend to buy your product, but never do. Sometimes they say it to get you off their backs. Sometimes, they intended to buy your product, but it was momentary, and they never really had a conviction about your product.

The second reason that purchase intent is not a measure of advertising effectiveness is that intent is formed by a variety of factors. The part played by advertising can't be identified, isolated and quantified.

The Right Answer

And now, the simple and correct answer. You know your agency is doing a good job for you if they are creating advertising which has a good likelihood of persuading people to change their minds in ways that favor your company. That's it.

Sure, there are other things you look for in an agency. There should be a close relationship between advertiser and agency. They should be smart, be enjoyable to work with and have integrity. They should listen to you.

These other evaluative criteria are important, but the most important criterion in selecting an agency should be its ability to produce advertising that works for you.

Get It Right Up Front

How do you and your agency create advertising that can accomplish this difficult task? Start by eliminating all those vacuous generalities people mouth when you ask them about a piece of advertising.

Answers usually involve things like, "It sure will get attention," "It's very creative," "It's really clever," "It's really funny," and the ever-popular "I like it, and so does the chairman of the board."

Ensure effective advertising by demanding it from the very beginning of the creative process. Before a word is written, identify the things that give advertising a greater likelihood of being effective, and use them to guide you as you develop the creative work.

If You Don't Stand for Something, You'll Fall for Anything

When we tell advertising practitioners their goal is to change minds and persuade by changing knowledge, beliefs and attitudes, we owe it to them to set out as specifically as possible how they can do that.

At some point, the advertising industry must emphatically state that the paramount advertising objective is to help persuade people by changing their knowledge, beliefs and attitudes.

It must develop a definition of effective advertising and specific standards with which to measure it. Everyone must agree on the basic evaluative criteria in determining what is likely to be effective and what isn't.

These standards must walk a fine line--specific enough so that everyone involved in the process, from creatives to clients, will understand them in the same way, yet not so narrow that imagination and innovation are stifled. The idea is to have everyone thinking effectiveness and persuasion.

Without writing volumes to cover every conceivable situation and question, we need to be clear in our intent and direction.

The objective is to get strong, bold, unusual, fascinating advertising. We do not want to constrain creatives and require that all advertising be selected from a list of approved creative formats. If the industry makes the goals clear, creative types will find exciting ways to make it happen.

Our task now is to determine which evaluative criteria should be used to identify effective advertising. Notice I didn't say that using these criteria will definitely result in more effective creative.

Nobody can guarantee the effectiveness of a piece of advertising. All we can do is identify factors which are usually related to effective advertising and try to create ads that take those factors into account.

Equally important, ads should be developed, reviewed and approved using a consistent set of criteria. If we ask our creative people to overlay the discipline of these criteria onto the creative process, we have to ask the clients who approve the ads to judge them accordingly.

Uncertainty Is Part of Advertising

You don't need statistics and research findings to have confidence in your advertising decisions. In the highly subjective world of advertising, you will always be making decisions under uncertainty, but that's not bad.

Before you object to the lack of statistical comfort and certainty with this approach, let's look at reality. Why do companies pay their top managers millions of dollars? Not for reading statistics and doing exactly what the data dictates. Managers get paid for making decisions under uncertainty.

If decisions can be made only after sufficient volumes of statistics remove all or almost all of the uncertainty, fire all the highly paid executives and replace them with supercomputers.

Ever seen a computer that needed a $10 million salary, stock options, stockholder-paid limo, expense account and corporate jet? Talk about saving money.

No matter how many numbers have been crunched or projections generated, there is seldom a certainty that an undertaking will be successful. With the prevailing "Let me entertain you" approach to advertising, everyone has to make creative decisions under uncertainty.

Focusing on effectiveness won't make uncertainty go away. It won't guarantee you will always make the right decisions. However, if you know and follow effectiveness-based evaluative criteria in the development process, you will have a better chance of changing minds than you do now.

Uncertainty is part of the rush you get in the advertising business. Advertising can be likened to betting on a horse race. At the track, you buy a racing form to see all the statistics and information.

How good is the horse at this distance? How many wins does the jockey have? It has been raining a lot, so is he a good mudder? What do the odds makers think of his chances? How did he do in his last race? These are evaluative criteria.

Whether it's Del Mar or Doyle Dayne, whether you're trying to choose the right horse or the right TV spot, you can't get away from evaluative criteria and decision making under uncertainty. They are forever linked.

Select your evaluative criteria carefully and make sure they relate to effectiveness. Then put your money down, get a good seat, and don't throw your ticket away until the race is official.

Don't Forget Common Sense

Sometimes you look at research statistics or opinions from others and something just doesn't sound right. Perhaps a little voice is telling you that you ought to go left, in spite of the numbers indicating a right turn.

One example is the beloved Aflac duck, which came out of the highly-regarded Kaplan Thaler Group in New York. According to an article by Ken Auletta in the March 28, 2005 issue of *The New Yorker*, five TV commercials were run by a focus group to see how the duck concept worked. It didn't. It came in fifth out of five.

The duck did have one big thing going for it. It was remembered at three times the average rate for insurance advertising. Bless the agency and the client for going with the duck. This feathery fellow has taken his rightful place along side such notables as Charlie the Tuna, the California Raisins, the Jolly Green Giant and the Budweiser Clydesdales.

The point here is that research data alone are not enough to make smart decisions. You don't have to do everything by the book or by the numbers. The right evaluative criteria and common sense will result in smarter decisions and more effective advertising than depending on a pile of numbers to do your thinking for you.

Is My Advertising Working?

Every advertiser asks this question. Every advertising agency should, but usually doesn't unless the client pushes it. Actually, there are three separate questions here:

Q1. Is my advertising having an effect on sales?

RESULTS → BIG PROMISE

It is impossible to say. Too many variables are in operation; you can't identify the effects of just one, even one as visible as advertising.

Q2. What parts of the advertising are responsible for the change? What are we doing right?

Again, it is very hard to say. In advertising, everything works together--copy, visuals, Big Promise, Big (creative) Idea, reasons to believe the Big Promise, the media strategy. It's a team game, and the team that has all the parts working together will win.

Q3. Is the concept I'm using getting better or worse results than other concepts would?

The only way to even come close to knowing is by doing paired comparison research studies, which are very expensive and not necessarily accurate. Otherwise, you'll never know.

In spite of the fact that these questions can't be answered with certainty, they are legitimate questions. Three truths will provide more complete answers to them.

Truth #1. Advertising does not make sales.

Salespeople, stores, catalogs and the Internet make sales. The job of advertising is to prepare the consumer's mind, to give the target audience the knowledge, beliefs and attitudes which will make a purchase more likely.

Once you realize that the objective of all advertising should be to help in the persuasion process, you know what you need to assess the effectiveness of advertising—knowledge, beliefs and attitudes.

One of the most common and egregious mistakes advertisers make is to assume that sales increases or decreases are directly related to advertising. This leads to another silly mistake which is assuming that advertising can provide a quick fix to sagging or lagging sales.

If sales slump, advertising is always one of the usual suspects. Ignoring the fact that there are many more powerful factors affecting results, advertisers zoom in on the advertising. Often they assume it is the problem, and that a new advertising concept may be the solution.

The right thing to do is make a complete inventory of all the things that might be causing the sagging sales, then use experience and common sense to identify the cause(s) and the remedies.

Truth #2. You can't separate and quantify the effect of each of the many factors that affect sales.

The four Ps of marketing are product, price, place (of distribution) and promotion. By far, the most powerful P is product. If you want to be successful, the first and foremost requirement is a product that delivers what people want or need.

Several factors affect the marketing equation. A change in any one of them may cause significant changes in results. Here are the commonly encountered factors:

- Competitive products
- Competitive pricing, including short-term changes like sales and coupons
- Competitive media strategies
- Competitive promotional activities (special events, promotions, public relations)

- Competitive advertising approach and/or activity by city, state and region
- Weather
- Media weight
- Uncontrollable disruptive events
- News which affects the product, company or industry
- Product availability (i.e. more retail outlets; new distribution channels added)
- Economic conditions (national, state, urban vs. rural, specific neighborhoods)
- Technology
- Evaluative criteria for the product category (i.e. design, miles per gallon)
- The target audience's knowledge, beliefs and attitudes
- Raw material price and availability

How can you know which factor or combination of factors is responsible for results being what they are? How can you know whether an effect is caused by factor A alone, or if factors B, C and Z have caused a change in factor A? You can't, because there are simply too many variables active at any one time.

Truth #3. No research strategy can provide accurate measurements and cross-analysis of all the factors.

Each variable has its own unit of measurement. You can't accurately compare the different units of measurement, so you can't identify how much of an increase or decrease is attributable to any one factor.

Advertising, just like every other part of the marketing mix, does not exist in a vacuum. In most companies of any significant size, advertising is planned and executed in parallel with other efforts to increase sales.

For example, it's not all that improbable that, in a two-month period, new ads will run, four sales reps will be added, a new price list will be adopted, and a major customer will have an upturn or downturn in their own sales. So how do you determine the impact of each item sales over these two months?

That's right, you can't, unless there is one overwhelming factor at work, such as a natural disaster. At any one time, most factors are actively exerting either positive or negative pressure on results. It is impossible to determine how much effect each of the factors is having on sales.

It is just like any team game. A football team has eleven men on the field at all times. No coach can tell you exactly how important each player is to the team. The effectiveness of one makes his teammates look more effective. The mistakes of one makes the others look less effective.

When someone asks you to relate sales directly to advertising, sit them down and calmly relate to them what you have just read. Don't ever let anyone tell you advertising effectiveness has a direct correlation with sales. It may or it may not, but you can never know for sure.

When you look at the variety of variables, it is obvious there are too many things going on to be able to make a reasonable estimate of the importance of each factor. It is tempting to draw a straight line between advertising and results, but it is impossible.

Proof That Accountability Is a Pipe Dream

It's hard for most business people to believe that you can't measure something. If you feel this way, there is one quick way to prove the utter futility of trying to identify the contribution of any one factor to the total sales increase or decrease.

The first step in assessing accountability is to define the portion of the total effect on sales that is attributable to each factor. Admittedly it is impossible to be accurate when two factors affect each other. For instance, if a TV ad campaign is used to introduce a great new product, how much credit is due each factor?

Here is a list of the factors that usually have the greatest impact on sales. Select a product, then indicate the relative importance of each factor that affects sales of this product by filling in the blanks. The total of all factors must add up to 100%.

How Important Is Each Factor?

1. Your product   _____%
2. Competitors' products   _____%
3. Your pricing   _____%
4. Competitors' pricing   _____%
5. Your packaging   _____%
6. Competitors' packaging   _____%
7. Your advertising   _____%
8. Competitors' advertising   _____%
9. Your media weight   _____%
10. Competitors' media weight   _____%
11. Your product placements   _____%
12. Competitors' product placements   _____%
13. Your promotions   _____%

14. Competitors' promotions	_____%
15. Your public relations	_____%
16. Competitors' public relations	_____%
17. Your distribution system	_____%
18. Competitors' distribution system	_____%
19. Your customer service	_____%
20. Competitors' customer service	_____%
21. Weather	_____%
22. Industry news	_____%
23. Surprise disruptive events	_____%
24. Technology	_____%
25. Economic conditions	_____%
26. Societal attitudes and social mores	_____%
27. Consumer needs and wants	_____%
TOTAL EFFECT	100 %

If you're confident enough in your ability to do this once, remember that you need to do it every time you analyze the pieces of your marketing program. Don't forget to estimate the extent to which each factor has changed since the last time.

Don't Hide Behind Numbers

I feel sorry for account managers and ad managers. Management puts so much pressure on them to generate numbers. Numbers which can be used to select the best ads. Numbers which show how effective the advertising is. Numbers which can give managers at all levels help and confidence in making and defending decisions about advertising.

Numbers give comfort to people because they cover their rear ends when things don't turn out well. Imagine how it must sound inside a top manager's head.

"Sales are down. We have to find someone or something to blame. Who has the worst numbers? It must be their fault. What, you have no numbers? What are you, some kind of a nut? Do some research on something so you can have numbers. That's only good management. You'll feel better. What am I thinking? It's the advertising. It's so visible, it has to be the problem. Get me the advertising research numbers. They will tell me who is to blame."

The Simple Answer

To determine the effectiveness of your advertising, all you have to do is ask a few simple questions. Ask them once before you conduct an advertising campaign.

Then ask them two or more times after the campaign has been completed. Do people know your Big Promise? Do they believe it? Do they know the specific things that make your product the best choice? Do they have positive attitudes toward your product and your company?

These are the things advertising can and should affect. This is what you need to measure.

Stop Advertising

Advertisers, especially top management, often question the usefulness of advertising. Many consider it a frill of questionable value; some see it as a total waste of money. In such cases, I have suggested to clients that they stop advertising. When faced with that decision, not one could imagine doing business without it.

I understand that, but wouldn't it be interesting to see what would happen to results if a company stopped advertising for a period of time, say three to six months?

This would be as valid a strategy as any for assessing the effect of advertising because it purposely changes only one factor. However, even though you are leaving all other variables under your control unchanged, the many factors over which you have no control can still cause changes in results.

Even if you stop advertising, you'll never really know the cause(s) of the results during the no-advertising time.

You Should Always Focus on the Same Objectives

The business world makes a big deal about objectives. If you don't have objectives, you're perceived to be a loser and a ne'er do well. I feel the need to weigh in on this issue.

Come on, admit it. Objectives, goals or whatever you call them, are nothing more than hopes and dreams. They are not sacred. When top management announces that the goal for the coming year is a ten percent sales increase, it means they want, desire or hope for a ten percent increase.

If you are in charge of advertising, what do sales goals mean to you? Nothing, absolutely nothing. You only have control over advertising, and advertising should always have the same objective – persuade as many people as possible to use your product by instilling in them the appropriate knowledge, beliefs and attitudes.

Is the advertising objective a ten percent sales increase? No. That's the corporate objective. Advertising objectives should be couched in terms of changing minds, that's all.

At some point, you have to assign a numerical value to your advertising objectives. You have to say that you want a five percent increase in the number of people who believe your product is the creamiest, the most powerful, the hippest, the most reliable.

Does that mean your advertising is underachieving or weak if you only get a three percent increase? No, it does not. It simply means you made some progress. Could it have been more? Perhaps, but it could have been less. One way to tell how you are doing is to measure changes in the scores of your competitors on the same questions.

You could also try to do paired comparisons to see if three percent is an acceptable figure. This is a very expensive process because it requires development and production of two different advertising campaigns. Very few companies are willing or able to do this.

This is how a paired comparison test might work. You take ten cities and pair each of them with another city that is similar in terms of sales volume, population, demographic composition, and product category activity. You run two different advertising campaigns, one in the ten base cities, the other in the ten comparable cities.

After the campaigns have run, you take measurements in all twenty cities, and compare results to see if one of the creative approaches is consistently superior at changing minds.

You would also want to see which advertising approach is related to the best sales results, but since there are so many other variables in play when looking at sales, this is not the important information. You want to know if advertising did the job specifically assigned to it, and that should always relate to changes in knowledge, beliefs and attitudes.

Chapter 7

PROBLEM #6: THEY'RE NOT USING RESEARCH CORRECTLY

Advertising is a soft business, dealing in ideas. Research is a hard business, dealing in numbers. It can drive creatives bonkers, but account management and clients feel more comfortable and confident when they have numbers to support their positions or actions. This is true whether they're putting together an advertising plan, a media buy or a piece of creative.

Advertising-related research provides information in several areas, as you can see below. This is a book about the creative product, so I'm going to deal only with the last two, the uses of research pertaining specifically to the creative execution.

- Demographics (age, sex, family status, income)
- Psychographics (lifestyle indicators)
- Product information (primary and competitive)
- Media usage (audience size & composition)
- Creative development (doing an effective ad)
- Creative impact (what happened?)

Research in the Creative Process - Development

Let's assume that research has been done to provide pertinent product, competitive and audience information. The first point at which research can help agencies and advertisers during the creative process is after initial copy and layout have been completed.

Discipline yourself to measure only those things advertising can directly affect – knowledge, beliefs and attitudes. Don't get caught up in measuring other things, like purchase intent or how much people like the ads. They aren't important.

Most advertisers and agencies use this research to determine which ad(s) will be produced. Another frequent use of this research is to test the viability of an ad which is the agency or client favorite.

You're Not Ready to Pick a Winner

This is initial creative research; it's too early to try to pick a winner at this point. Use this research to identify areas for improvements that could improve the ads' persuasive strength. Research at this point should seek to find anything in the proposed creative work that might get in the way of clear communication. You should be looking for potential problems. Use the research information to identify changes that will make the creative work harder toward the objectives.

Go Beneath the Surface

Don't dismiss little things quickly. What sounds trivial or off-base may be important. You can't always take comments at face value. Sometimes little things are related to and lead to other, larger issues that people can't easily verbalize. Take time to ask why your research subjects feel like they do. Ask them how they suggest dealing with the problem. Don't be afraid to challenge them.

Toward the end of focus group sessions, researchers often ask a question like, "Would this ad make you more likely to buy the product?" It is a useless question. People will tell you what they think you want to hear, and they probably won't do what they tell you they are going to do.

It's easy to assume that ads which people like will make them more likely to buy the product. This is not necessarily true. In some cases, liking the ad and feeling good about the advertiser are enough to affect purchase behavior. In most cases, they are not.

People aren't stupid. They want to make smart buys, and they appreciate and use both emotional and factual information to make a decision.

Does an ad give them new and useful information? Does it change their attitudes or beliefs? If so, why? These are the things you need to know.

Round Two

After revisions have been made and the agency and client have narrowed the options to two or three serious contenders, there are two possibilities.

First, a second round of consumer research could be conducted to see if the changes have been improvements or just changes. The other option is to analyze the revised work and, if everyone is in agreement, select the work to be produced.

Whatever the decision-making process, don't ever use research data to select a winner. Advertising involves a wide variety of feelings, beliefs and attitudes. It isn't easy, perhaps not even possible, for statistics to accurately reflect this.

You hire an ad agency for its sense of what will be persuasive. You pay them a lot of money for their expertise. Don't let the perceived safety and accuracy of statistics lure you into the trap of using data to make decisions.

Researchers get paid for providing data to help you in making decisions. Managers get paid for making decisions under uncertainty, which certainly describes advertising.

Measuring Creative Impact

Now for the second point at which research is used during the creative process. The ads have been produced and their scheduled run in the media has been completed. This is where you try to find out if they had the desired impact on the target audience.

This is done with a simple three-step process using the pre- and post-exposure research format.

1. Before the new advertising appears, conduct a survey of the target audience's knowledge, beliefs and attitudes. Include questions that probe the status of both your company or client and competitors.

2. Expose your audience to the advertising.

3. Using the exact same questions and research protocol, conduct one or more follow-up surveys to measure changes in knowledge, beliefs and attitudes. Questions should be specific to these areas, and should not track superficial issues like awareness and recall.

Notice that I suggest the possibility of more than one follow-up survey. It is not enough to do one post-schedule survey. It takes a while for people to see, understand and internalize input. Don't panic if your first post-schedule survey doesn't show a big shift. You should do at least one or two more surveys to track changes over time.

If resources are available, it is best to conduct follow-up surveys on a regular schedule. This keeps you current with the market and helps prevent nasty surprises.

Not only will this tell you if your message is getting across, it also will tell you when you have made enough impact, so you can back off or change messaging in your advertising. This can prevent wasting money by telling people what they already know or don't care about.

Research Options

The type of information and predictive ability of the research data depend on selecting the right research protocol. Depending on the situation, you might select phone survey, mall intercept survey, on-air test, Internet survey, laboratory test, or focus group. Let's check to ensure we're talking the same language. Here is a quick definition of each research format.

Phone

The research equivalent of telemarketing. Sometimes people are selected at random, sometimes on specific factors. In either case, people give responses during a phone survey that lasts for several minutes.

Mall Intercept

People are "intercepted" while walking around the mall, asked to look at some advertising and answer questions about it. This is better than a phone survey because they actually see the advertising.

On-Air

Ads are placed in regular TV or radio programming, then a phone survey is done to measure recall of the commercial and reactions to it.

Internet & E-mail

The Internet is a smart option for many research requirements. It has a couple of shortcomings when it comes to testing creative. First, participants must be able to see the materials they are asked to analyze. Not all people have computers.

Also, not all computers have enough bandwidth to allow playing of TV spots, which eliminates part of the population from participation in this format.

Second, spontaneous follow-up questions and discussions are an important part of creative testing. The Internet and e-mail are not very easy ways to do this because they do not allow the easy and rapid give and take of face-to-face interaction.

Laboratory Test

A format gaining in availability and popularity. Groups of about 20-50 in size are gathered in a specially wired room at a research firm. They are shown advertising, usually TV spots, and asked to register their response by using an electronic device which has a big dial on it. Turn it to the right if you like something or some part of the commercial, left if you don't like something.

A moderator usually shows pieces of advertising and leads the discussion. This method is good for identifying specific parts of the spot to which people strongly react.

Focus Groups

Of all the available research tools, focus groups have an exalted status among agencies and advertisers. While focus groups have their value, they also have many pitfalls.

A focus group usually includes 8-12 people from the desired target audience, gathered around a conference table at a research firm or other neutral location. Clients and agency personnel view them through a one-way mirror.

A moderator usually shows pieces of advertising and leads the discussion. Participants typically get free food and non-alcoholic beverages, and are paid for their two hours of attendance.

Focus Group Foibles

Focus groups are used for just about any research where you want to hear from the public. They are very popular because they are relatively easy and inexpensive to put together, the client and agency can watch them live, and it is assumed that these people somehow are representative of, and speak for, the general public.

Beware of putting too much credence in focus group results. For one thing, the actions of the moderator can be a big problem. Moderators are professional researchers, and often have only a superficial knowledge of the product, the market, the marketing situation and the creative process. They work off a sheet of prepared questions, and may not be able to probe deeply for important additional information.

Second, participants frequently want to please and thank the sponsors for the free food/drink and money, so some of them tend to say what they think the advertiser wants to hear.

Third, one strong personality can skew a group to the point that the information gathered is useless. These people come in all shapes and sizes, but can intimidate and/or pull the whole group into accepting their opinions.

Fourth, clients and ad agencies will often use the limited information from a couple of groups to make important decisions, such as selecting the creative concept to be used. Somehow, seeing people live gives their opinions great credibility with those corporate voyeurs behind the one-way glass.

They Are Only Numbers

A big challenge in advertising is how to use research properly. So it doesn't send you down the wrong path. So it doesn't put your creative work in a straightjacket. So it doesn't make your decision for you. So it does give you knowledge to make informed decisions.

To a lot of people the term "research findings" means the same thing as evidence, truth or facts. We see that forty-two percent of the people preferred commercial A and thirty-nine percent preferred B, and we anoint A the superior spot.

In our zeal to pick a winner, we often forget there is an error factor in most research, usually in the range of plus or minus five percent. If the research gives a score of forty-two percent, the real number could be anywhere from thirty-seven percent to forty-seven percent.

Just because a few members of the public like an ad does not mean it is going to be effective. These people don't have any idea what makes an ad effective. All they know is what they like, which means they will probably go for clever, humorous ads, regardless of the quality of the message or lack thereof.

Advertising research isn't infallible. More frequently than we want to admit, it is used to cover the behind of everyone in the process and pass the blame for poor performance to the research or the public. Whenever you are looking at research data, use common sense when you decide what the research data are really saying.

A Bold Recommendation

Formal research isn't a slam dunk in terms of providing all the right answers. Statistics are not a substitute for broad perspective thinking, experience, an intuitive understanding of people and plain old gut feel. They are all helpful in making an informed decision.

As Rod Serling used to say on *The Twilight Zone*, "I offer for your consideration..." - a unique possibility, to be used as either a substitute for standard formal research techniques or in conjunction with them.

It is simply this. The ad agency of record asks another advertising agency to review objectives, creative brief and ad materials for the project, and critique them. Here's how it works:

1. An agency establishes a reciprocal, contractual relationship with three or four good agencies in different cities, preferably in different parts of the country.

2. The agencies chosen should share a commitment to and use of the principles of effective advertising.

3. As needed, the agency sends proposed ad materials, pertinent information and a list of questions and issues to one (or more) of the other agencies.

4. The receiving agency analyzes and critiques the materials, asking questions during the process.

5. The receiving agency sends a written response to the requesting agency, which may be followed by Q & A sessions.

6. The requesting agency pays the receiving agency the prearranged amount.

I know this a radical proposal. It involves extra work. It costs money. It takes time. You are showing your creative work to other agencies. You know better than any other agency what is best for your client.

All true, but wouldn't it be smart, if your agency ego can take it, to have an impartial expert opinion to help you stay on the path to effective advertising?

Chapter 8

PROBLEM #7: THEY PRODUCE ONEZIES, NOT CAMPAIGNS

A lot of advertisers, including big ones, aren't creating cohesive, long-lasting campaigns. Nobody ever talks about this as a problem, and it may not sound like a big deal, but it is.

Instead they are producing "onezies". Onezies are individual ads from one advertiser which don't look or sound like other ads from advertiser. They may use the same tag line, but are not otherwise similar. There is no consistent big idea, just a bunch of unconnected little ideas.

The term onezie doesn't mean they run only once. It means the ad is one of a kind, not part of a coordinated, ongoing campaign. In contrast, a campaign consists of multiple ads that share the same Big Promise, same reasons to believe the Big Promise, same creative approach and same basic structure and format.

What's the Big Idea?

So what's the big deal about continuity and a Big Idea? To begin with, a Big Idea is the creative approach you take to deliver and support your Big Promise. It could be a visual cue, spokesperson, format, music or demonstration technique.

It's a look, a feel, a format; something that people can use to immediately identify the advertising as belonging to the advertiser. Think of it as something that reminds people of the Big Promise without seeing or hearing the whole ad.

Campaigns Are More Effective

Campaigns which feature a consistent format and messaging are much more effective than onezies. For one thing, it takes a while for people to realize and remember the messages in advertising.

You run advertising multiple times to give people time to go through the process which ideally ends with them understanding the messages and knowing the name of the sponsor

When you use the same Big Idea and the same format to deliver the same Big Promise, all three things are reinforced each time a person sees, hears or reads an ad.

The Big Idea helps people recall prior exposures to an ad or ad campaign whenever they are exposed to it again. This reinforces the messages and product or corporate positioning.

Also, when people see or hear an ad consistent in format and main message with prior ads, they can more readily attribute it to a specific company or product. This allows them to better focus on the message.

No Continuity, No Memorability

With onezies, people have to pay so much attention to the new creative idea that they aren't able to focus on the message. With onezies, there is no reinforcement, no imprinting, no increased memorability of prior advertising.

On the contrary, the person has to remember new things, which means a lot of what the person has remembered from the prior ads will no longer be reinforced, and will be more easily forgotten. Onezies are a more costly and less effective way to advertise.

Why Do People Create Onezies?

Even faced with the clear benefits of doing a consistent campaign, onezies are still produced, for three reasons:

1. Boredom. Clients and agencies spend a lot of time developing and producing advertising. They go over every part of a piece of advertising so many times, by the time the ad is finished, it's no longer fresh and fun for them. It's old hat, so those involved already are looking ahead to the next creative project. With this mindset, it's easy for agencies, and clients as well, to press for production of new ads.

2. The second factor is the self-serving desire by advertising agencies to produce as many new ads as possible. It generates profits while providing more ads which may be award-winners in creative competitions. There is a desire to create something totally new, not just a different take on what has already been produced.

3. As unlikely as it seems, there are clients and agencies who don't realize the value of consistency in advertising. I can't imagine this is a prevalent situation, but if you know someone who fits this description, buy them a copy of this book.

Television Message Recall Test

To understand the difficulty of the customer connecting message and messenger, try this test.

1. Spend a half hour watching TV or listening to the radio.

2. Turn off the TV or radio and wait ten minutes.

3. Write down the names of all the sponsors you can remember from the half hour.

4. Now write down what you remember about each sponsor's spot, focusing on major messages or customer benefits.

You might want to get friends, family and co-workers to take the test too. Don't worry if you aren't able to remember many sponsors, and even fewer messages. Not many people can.

While there are no reliable statistics for this test, I would be surprised if you are able to remember more than three or four sponsors and one or two messages. Once you have taken this test, you will understand why it takes time, consistent messaging and an interesting format to generate a memorable message.

Chapter 9

PROBLEM #8: THE APPROVAL PROCESS IS MEANINGLESS

When something is approved, there is an implied covenant between the approver and the people who will use that which has been approved. If the health inspector approves the little Thai restaurant down the block, they are telling us we can count on having some Pad Thai without getting food poisoning.

If we buy a TV set that has UL listed wiring, we assume the set won't explode and burst into flames because of faulty wiring. We assume that the "approval" means something.

When it comes to advertising, approval only means that the person approving an ad accepts it as something they like. There is no implied warranty or guarantee of effectiveness, and no assurance that it will do the job it is expected to do.

The approved ad hasn't had to meet any standards. It hasn't been analyzed according to commonly-accepted criteria for effectiveness. Approval of an ad just means that the approver has a feeling that the ad is good. I think this qualifies as a meaningless approval process.

The Approvers Are Dangerous

The people who have the final approval of advertising can be very dangerous to their advertising programs. No, they aren't going to break your knee caps if they don't like the creative. The danger is much more subtle. The danger is that the most effective advertising may never be seen by the target audience. These people are dangerous for three reasons:

1. They don't understand what advertising is supposed to do.
2. They don't know effective from ineffective advertising. They just know what they like.
3. They don't know what has been going on during the creative development in the preceding weeks or months.

Who are these people? For a very small client, there is usually one approver, probably the owner. As you move up in size, you add a manager responsible for marketing and advertising, so now you have two or three levels of approval.

As company size increases, more people get involved, usually some mix of division managers, regional sales managers, product managers, brand managers and directors and VPs of marketing. Each one has input and a somewhat informed opinion.

Opinions Are Free

The one thing these people share is little or no real understanding of advertising. People who haven't had any advertising effectiveness training, and who have had little or nothing to do with the planning or development process are able to only offer their opinions.

These people often have absolutely no idea what they should be looking for, or what evaluative criteria to use. They only have opinions. These are not stupid people. They are intelligent, motivated executives who get paid a lot of money to know things, have informed opinions and make tough decisions.

When they are asked to review advertising and render an opinion, by golly, they're going to have opinions and make decisions.

A Penchant for the Negative

When you want an outside opinion on something, what kind of a person do you seek - someone who talks only about the good things or someone who is more skeptical and analytical?

I want someone who is looking for mistakes, who digs and asks tough questions like a cop interrogating a suspect. I want someone who assumes there are flaws, and earnestly wants to find them.

Executives know that if they find fault, it adds to their status and credibility, so they'll try to find things wrong. That would be fine if they knew what to look for, if they knew creative right from wrong. But these people don't know the important difference between clever and creative, between entertainment and effective advertising.

They see a clever play on words or hear a funny radio spot and think it is great advertising, despite the lack of any product message.

Everyone Is an Expert

There's an old saying that everyone thinks they're an advertising expert. Have you ever stopped to think what that really means? You don't hear that said about other professions. How would you feel if everyone thought they were a dermatologist or a structural engineer?

You go to professionals because they have expertise, training, knowledge and capabilities you don't have. When they tell you something, you believe it and accept their recommendations.

You don't tell your dentist how to do a root canal, your CPA how to do taxes, your acupuncturist where to put the needles, your dry cleaner how to get that stain out.

When it comes to advertising, however, clients routinely question and disagree with their agencies. They feel quite comfortable telling their agencies what is right and wrong. They tell their agencies how to do it.

They make decisions based on what they feel and think, rather than following recommendations of the advertising experts whom they hire, and to whom they pay a lot of money. Why?

Two things account for this unusual relationship between advertiser and ad agency. First, there is no commonly accepted definition of good advertising, no consistent set of criteria by which advertising quality is evaluated.

In the absence of strong direction, it all comes down to personal preference. The client's opinion is as good as the agency's opinion because opinion is the operative evaluative criteria.

Second, there are so few agency people with any in-depth advertising training and knowledge. Many agency account managers and creative team members are not capable of forming a logical, reasoned, credible argument in support of their beliefs.

They can't point to a body of research or case studies that give credible support for why the agency did what it did. All they have is their opinions, usually based on personal feelings and preferences.

When a client and an agency have opposing opinions and philosophies about advertising, the fact that the client has the money and the power to fire the agency weighs heavily in the decision.

Top Guns Are Conservative.

Now let's go right to the top. The CEO, COO, president, and chairman of the board may have the final approval of advertising. They should. Advertising is extremely visible, reflects on the company, and, in the absence of public relations efforts, may be the only thing people see about the company.

Top managers are usually the most careful, conservative people in the approval chain. They worry about things like liability, ROI, stock price, corporate image, and what the guys at the country club will think.

When it comes to advertising, they generally are not risk-takers, and will opt for what they think is the safe choice. This can be a problem. The proliferation of advertising makes it hard to stand out amid the clutter. How do you stand out and get your message heard?

The way I look at it, if everyone else is going right, go left. Be different, bold, unusual, unexpected. If you're not trying to do this, you are missing a lucrative opportunity to gain an edge over the competition.

The top managers probably know little or nothing about what they're being asked to approve, which makes them even more conservative, and more dangerous. Because they have had little, if any connection with the advertising creation, they need to see research results and statistics before rendering an opinion.

You can't blame them for wanting to educate themselves; these are important decisions. What did customers think of the advertising? What do the numbers say about which commercial is best? This is why ad managers do research.

Effective advertising is bold, powerful, arresting, possibly unique, and at times controversial. It also makes top management nervous, and will often get the thumbs down if the final approver hasn't been properly prepared and informed by the marketing and advertising group.

What Clients Can Do

Clients, when you review advertising for approval, make your agency show the proposed advertising in context. Always look at advertising in the environment in which it will be received.

This in-context presentation should not be an option. It allows you to more accurately assess the ability of the advertising to deliver your message and be effective in the face of all the competing advertising and promotion going on in the medium. It's the way your target audience will receive the ads. Press for the most effective advertising; don't just rubber stamp and fawn over whatever the agency brings you.

Both you and the agency should want effective advertising. If the agency hasn't brought you effective stuff, now is the time to determine that. This is best done by seeing it in somewhat the same over-communicated, confusing setting your advertising will encounter in the real world.

Presentation of the proposed creative work should not be prefaced by detailed explanations of objectives and rationale. Your customers and potential customers out there don't have that available; all they have is the ad. You can't explain the idea to your target audience, so it shouldn't be explained to you. It creates an unreal situation which facilitates bad decisions.

Just have the agency say hello, set up their equipment, and show the advertising. No other conversation should be allowed until all ads have been presented.

This is done because most people will hear an ad several times, and it takes more than once to even begin to understand a lot of advertising, especially broadcast spots.

What Agencies Can Do

Account managers at all levels, resist the temptation and tendency to sell the advertising, to try to convince your client it is good and should be approved. Creatives tell you that your job is to get the advertising approved. It isn't. **Your job is to make your client's advertising as effective as possible.**

Print ads should be put into appropriate publications rather than beautifully mounted on black card stock. Paste your proposed magazine or newspaper ad in a full issue of the publication, hand it to the client and say, "Your ad is in here."

Radio spots and TV spots should be presented as part of a series of commercials, not by themselves. I suggest you put your proposed spot in among five spots from other advertisers. It's best if the new spot is somewhere in the middle.

If you're wondering what kind of spots the five placebos should include, they should be from well-known, national quality products. For one thing, they are your competition for space in the consumer's mind. Also, national spots tend to have higher production values and creative concepts.

To encourage your agency to do its best, you have to set the bar high. A lot of mediocre spots can test well against bad local work, but who wants mediocre advertising?

For brochures or mailing pieces, hand your client a group of 8-10 well-produced pieces, putting the item being presented toward the end of the group.

For outdoor signage, don't mount the proposed board on a black background so it's all the client sees. Select a colored photograph of an urban or suburban setting, blow it up and blur it a little.

Cover the presentation board completely with the enlarged, blurred background photo and put your proposed board in the upper half of it, not necessarily centered.

Have your client close their eyes, place the board in front of them, then say "Open". Count to three, then put the board face down on the table. Repeat this two more times, then ask the client to tell you what they saw.

What if the client doesn't remember it? If that happens, there may be something wrong with the creative. To prevent such ghastly surprises, do several practice runs with people in the agency or friends who haven't worked on the project. If the board isn't well remembered, it's a sign that this board has little or no chance to be effective in the real world.

Preparing for Executive Approvals

Ad managers and agency account managers, do not treat lightly the final approval by top managers. When these folks say no to advertising you have planned and overseen, guess who gets the blame? No, it's not the creatives. It's you.

Worse yet, they may be giving the heave-ho to effective advertising just because they don't like the size of the logo, the color of the shirt or the use of a word.

Remember that you and the top brass are generally coming from different directions. You should be pushing for bold, powerful, industry-changing communication. Honchos prefer things that aren't innovative or controversial.

It's a big job, but clients hire ad agencies to push the envelope, so do your homework, be unusual as you deliver a powerful product message, and be bold in your creative and your defense of it.

To increase the chances that justice will be done to the creative product, you have to prepare for the final approval session. Don't just pop your head in the big wheel's office and ask if he or she has a minute to look at some advertising. Remember, this is the final step in the creative process, a time when ads can be weakened or killed.

Here's what you do. Make an appointment, then send an email and hard copy memo which includes a backgrounder with summary information on...

1. The specific reason for the meeting (i.e. review and approval of two new TV spots)
2. The marketing/advertising situation that led to this creative work
3. Objectives of this advertising
4. Competitive advertising activity
5. Research done & key results
6. Big promise
7. Big idea (creative format & its history)
8. Summary media plan
9. Recap of the last three years' advertising
10. The list of evaluative criteria

Dear Big Wheels

Client top managers, do your organization and yourself a favor and spend some time with your advertising before deciding which way to point your thumb. Take time to understand what effective advertising is, what the objectives and strategies are, and what the agency and your people say.

Don't use advertising approval time to overcome your lack of understanding of the advertising world. Here are some things to avoid. Keep these in mind and you will get more effective advertising.

- Don't "hold court." This is not the time for you to pontificate on your philosophy about advertising and marketing. A lot of work has been done. Respect it.

- Don't come in cold. Read the backgrounder so you know what is needed from you, and so you can make intelligent decisions.

- Don't use vague words, like good, bad, creative or cute. Make specific reference to visuals and copy that you question.

- Don't say "I like it" or "I don't like it". Talk in specifics that relate to the likelihood of effectiveness. Consult your list of evaluative criteria

- Don't suggest changes in wording or visuals unless you have a specific practical reason you believe strongly will increase the effectiveness of the advertising. Personal preferences or practices don't qualify.

- Don't get into extraneous discussions about advertising theory or your concern that a competitor has a funnier campaign. This meeting has a specific purpose.

Make Approvals Mean Something

A lot of time, effort and money goes into development of advertising. Don't treat the approval as a necessary evil; it's your last chance to give your work every opportunity to do the difficult assignment you have given it.

Arm the approver with the right criteria, anticipate questions and objections, and know the answers. It's embarrassing when the corporate president rejects your ad based on the appropriate evaluative criteria; it's a lot worse to have your bad advertising seen by the target audience.

Chapter 10

PROBLEM #9: ADVERTISING'S DRUG OF CHOICE—AWARDS.

Awards are an extremely important part of the advertising business. Award-winning advertising is used by the industry to define what good advertising looks and sounds like.

Attempts to get agencies excited about effective advertising will face tough sledding unless award shows use more specific evaluative criteria which relate to effectiveness, and not to appearance, cleverness or humor value.

I have noted a consistency in the kind of ads that have been winning awards over the years. This is a powerful indication that the award shows encourage and reward the development of a certain style of advertising.

Don't get me wrong. I don't think the award shows have done this intentionally. The fine people who run the various shows have high standards and the best intentions.

The award shows don't have an agenda to control creative, it just happens. Many shows publish and sell books to show the industry who and what ads won that year. The creative departments in advertising agencies take it from there.

Creatives frequently consult the award show books, *HOW* magazine and *Communication Arts* magazine as they work on a project. They scan through the winning ads to see which agencies and which people are getting awards. Naturally, they want to see what the winners look like. They also are on the lookout for concepts, formats or Big Ideas they can adapt for use in their work.

I enjoy looking at these books. It's fun to see who and what is winning. I salute the talented, dedicated creatives for doing award-winning advertising. I have won forty-two awards in creative competitions, and it really makes a person feel good.

Most creatives aren't looking to steal ideas from these books. They are looking for inspiration, direction, something to spark their creativity. If you have a strong desire to win awards, you have to see what is winning.

The end result, however, is that there is a strong tendency to do work that has an appearance, tone of voice and feel similar to previous award winners.

The award shows have a powerful say in the look and feel of advertising, but they are not bad guys. They just have a desirable product that has the ability to control the industry.

These Are Criteria?

I don't have a problem with the award shows per se. My concern is with the evaluative criteria being used in these competitions, or rather the lack of them. The judging criteria are so vague that they can be construed to mean almost anything. It comes down to the individual creative philosophies of the judges.

Without identifying the specific shows, here are the judging criteria now being used by the biggest, most prestigious creative competitions in the world:

"The creativity of the work"

"Distinctive and memorable, coupled with achieving good business results."

"Sets new standards in communication thinking."

"To honor creativity in advertising."

"The year's most innovative creative work."

"To honor advertising and design excellence."

"To set industry standards for creative excellence."

"Great ideas that are well executed."

"Celebrate the creative accomplishments of smaller creative companies."

"To recognize distinction in creative work"

"Marketing effectiveness and creative execution."

These "What we look for" lists are so vague and subjective that they give no direction at all. Usually with no demonstrable interest in the effectiveness of ads, these shows become beauty contests. By default, the evaluative criteria become cleverness, humor value and slick looks.

We're Rewarding the Wrong Thing

In most competitions, you reward the activity that is the basis of the effort. In weightlifting, it's who lifts the most weights. Not who looks the beefiest or has the best grunts. In auto racing, it's who crosses the finish line first, not who has the fanciest paint job or the best looking driver. In gymnastics, it's who does the most difficult routine and makes the fewest errors. Unitard color and haircut are trivial.

It is different in advertising. Companies advertise with the expectation it will help bring about a result of some sort. Logic would tell you that advertising competitions would honor ads that helped bring about a result. So much for logic. Go back and look at the evaluative criteria of the various creative shows. You just can't put your finger on what they're rewarding.

That is my problem with ad shows. These shows aren't honoring ads that do the best job for clients. They're honoring ads for reasons only advertising professionals think are important.

As I have stated before, the primary job of advertising is to help persuade people to establish, reinforce or change their habits by changing their knowledge, beliefs and attitudes. So, it makes no sense that the vague evaluative criteria used in advertising shows focus on creativity, on the clever words, the beautiful visuals, the artistry of it all. It makes no sense that it's a beauty contest.

A lot of time is spent on account planning, account management, competitive analysis, media analysis, branding planning, research, setting of objectives and strategies, writing creative briefs and goodness knows what else. All designed to make the advertising as effective as possible.

This coordinated effort by many people means squat if the creative execution doesn't have the ability to change minds. Shouldn't advertising awards recognize the whole effort? Shouldn't advertising be recognized that does the job it has always been asked to do?

Award-Winners Aren't Necessarily Effective

Having followed award-winners for some time now, I have seen first hand that winning ads have had a remarkable consistency decade after decade. Winning ads for all media tend to be simple, nicely designed, humorous, and have little copy. The similarity of format over time indicates to me that form is more important than substance.

This kind of consistency makes you wonder if the evaluative criteria of the judges have more to do with hipness, humor and good looks than effectiveness. After all, there is no reason to think that highly effective ads would look alike.

Many of the ads that win awards in these competitions would probably win in effectiveness-based competitions. It is certainly possible, and definitely desirable, to be humorous, good looking, hip and effective at the same time.

It is not a stretch to suggest that award-winning advertising isn't necessarily effective advertising. It may be effective, but it may just be clever, funny or good looking. Given the consistently large number of humorous ads and the even larger number of small copy ads that win awards, one can make a compelling case that the award shows are responsible for perpetuating the development of ineffective advertising.

A Big Boost for Effective Advertising

Once effectiveness and persuasiveness become integral parts of the judging criteria, award shows will be a powerful force in establishing effectiveness as the objective, and the specific evaluative criteria as the operative strategies.

It is probably asking too much to have the major award shows immediately accept effectiveness-based evaluative criteria as the basis for their judging. More likely, shows may add another category, where judging is based on effectiveness criteria.

However it begins, there must be a transition to effectiveness criteria such as those included in S.T.E.P. (Strategies & Tactics for Effective Persuasion) on page 157. It will take a few years, but it will come. As these criteria become known to the business world, advertisers will come to require that their agencies use them. As more agencies produce work based on these criteria, more ads of this type will be entered in competitions, and they will win.

At some point, the award shows may be encouraged by the sheer volume of entries to acknowledge the importance of effective advertising, and give the relevant criteria their rightful place in the shows.

Who Is to Blame?

Advertising award shows honor the creatives, but creative directors, copywriters and art directors aren't the people in the industry who value creative awards. They aren't the only ones who want the statues and recognition.

Creatives covet awards, but who would begrudge them a few statuettes, mentions in award show books, and peer approval? Give them their due. Creative is the product of this business.

Advertisers also are big on awards. They want their agencies to do award-winning ads. Why not? Awards are the only tangible, visible proof that an agency does great work. That is a very important evaluative criterion when selecting an agency. Nothing else involving impartial third party judgment is available when evaluating an agency.

Many advertisers are absolutely addicted to awards, convinced that they are an infallible indicator of a great agency. They want and expect their agency to win awards. What are agency managers to do?

What to Do About It

Creative awards are extremely important to everyone in the industry. If the awards competitions can be persuaded to include effectiveness in their evaluative criteria, the shows will be a huge asset to the industry.

Awards will still be the drug of choice in the industry, but if the competitions honor ads which try to be effective rather than just entertaining, the toughest battle will have been won.

Alert Agencies Will Prosper

Advertising agencies who only promote the hardware they have won in creative competitions are missing a bet. Once again, common sense will lead you to the truth. Three options exist for agencies trying to impress a potential client, or even an existing one. The correct option is clear.

Agency Focus	Likely Client Reaction
Creative awards	But does their stuff sell?
Results for clients	Was advertising totally responsible for results?
Creative awards based on effectiveness	These people can make us more successful

Agencies that talk about how they create work to get results for their clients will win more than their share of new clients. The reason? **Clients want results more than they want awards.**

Chapter 11

PROBLEM #10: THEY DON'T TRAIN THEIR PEOPLE

Anyone Can Call Themselves an Ad Professional

Advertising is one of the few professions you can enter without providing any proof of competency. Most professionals have to undergo some sort of accreditation process. There's usually a course of study and training, followed by a qualification test. You have to meet specified requirements and pass tests before you can call yourself a professional.

Doctors and dentists, lawyers and landscape designers, musicians and massage therapists, architects and accountants, realtors, beauticians and optometrists. They all have to give some kind of indication that they know a decent amount about their field before they are allowed to practice their crafts.

Then there's advertising. Get some business cards and a cell phone. Bam, you're an ad agency. We have no barriers to entry into the field. We let everyone in. Anyone can be an advertising professional.

Being Smart Isn't Enough

I don't think the advertising business is populated with clueless dummies. On the contrary, advertising professionals are a talented, well-educated group.

Account managers typically have college degrees, and sometimes a master's. They typically majored in marketing and/or advertising. Copywriters usually have some college-level education; many have college degrees. Art directors have had specialized schooling in their craft.

These people are smart, curious, clever, creative and fun to be around. It's not intelligence or education they lack, it is specific advertising expertise. Account managers have taken all the usual college advertising and marketing courses. Unfortunately, only a few universities offer a class in how to be an account executive.

I don't think there was a decent text book on account management until Don Dickinson wrote *The New Account Manager*, which I consider the definitive book on the greatly under-appreciated and very demanding task of account handling.

Yes, these people have formal education, but they aren't getting the right training once they get into the real world. The industry standard is on-the-job training, a polite way of saying no formal training. Oh, sure, some agencies may give new account execs some training, perhaps send them to a seminar or two, but not much of that sticks in the daily whirr.

What little training they may get is virtually useless. Sorry, but those day-long seminars, while well-meaning and offering good information, aren't enough to counter the lessons taught by daily real world experiences.

Once these new account managers get into the daily grind, they see how things are really done. Not surprisingly, they emulate their mentors, who learned the same way when they started out.

On the client side, it can get even worse. Once a person gets into an advertising position at an advertiser, there's virtually no chance of meaningful training. Funny how a person can become an instant expert when they are anointed the organization's advertising person.

Regrettably and predictably, when a person ascends to a position of perceived or assumed expertise, they believe they are an expert, that their ideas, preferences and judgments are correct. In an industry with no real standards of excellence and no understanding of the job of advertising, this leads to ineffective advertising.

In the absence of meaningful training, everyone is on their own. This leaves us with a lot of different definitions of good advertising, of what advertising is supposed to do. There are a lot of untrained, unprepared people out there, giving advice and creating advertising for clients who are putting their jobs and their companies' futures in the hands of these so-called professionals.

On the client side, we have managers, who usually know less than the agency, approving the advertising. Yeah, that's a big problem, but is it the biggest? Don't answer yet.

I'm Just an Ad Man Who Can't Say No

The biggest problem is that the industry is afraid to set limits, afraid to suggest that some things might be wrong, ineffective, counterproductive or stupid. Because there is an element of art in advertising, advertising practitioners refuse to have strong guidelines or, heaven forbid, rules which might make advertising more effective. For one thing, they might appear to limit the creative options and that would offend the creatives.

The result is that the advertising industry has no standards of excellence or execution. No commonly accepted idea of what is right and what is wrong. No demonstrated interest in carrying out advertising's mission to help persuade by changing knowledge, beliefs and attitudes.

With this vacuum of philosophy, direction and leadership, everyone who has a couple of years of experience becomes an advertising expert. The real-world learning which advertising rookies get, and which forms the bulk of their philosophies and work habits, comes from people who only knew what they were told by people, who only knew what they were told, who only knew what they were told, ad infinitum.

Passing on Ineptitude

Experienced advertising people don't realize they are dispensing uninformed and ill-informed advice, perpetuating the creation of weak, ineffective advertising. They strut through their advertising life, thinking they are God's gift to creativity, having not the tiniest hint that they are a major part of a major problem.

To be fair, there are people in the business who learn from their experiences and eventually waste less of their clients' money. Much of the time, unfortunately, they consider themselves an advertising expert, and they stop asking questions and trying new approaches.

We Need True Professionals

You don't get high-quality advertising without high-quality people. Advertising needs to set some barriers to entry into the business, so only people who thoroughly understand, buy into and are capable of carrying out the concept of effective advertising are allowed to practice.

The industry should also see to it that advertising professionals are well-trained throughout their careers. Lest you think training is a one-time deal for the wide-eyed, fresh-faced college grads, let's understand right now that everyone who plans, creates, presents and approves advertising needs periodic training. On the advertiser side and the ad agency side.

Just because a person passes a test to get into the business does not mean they will remember or practice what they learned. Periodic re-certification courses and tests should be given, to update and refresh one's knowledge base.

It Should Be No Picnic

How tough should it be to become certified and be allowed to practice advertising? This is an opportunity for the industry to get some badly needed credibility. It shouldn't be easy. Not everyone should pass. If everyone were to pass, it would render the certification process meaningless.

Certification should be granted only to people who have successfully completed tough training courses and passed a difficult final examination. To become a truly knowledgeable advertising professional, there is a lot to know in a lot of different areas. The certification process should include areas such as...

Advertising philosophy	Advertising planning
Account management	Ad relationships
Legal & ethical issues	The creative process
Creative briefs	Broadcast production
Print production	Presenting creative

Who Needs Certification?

The advertising industry includes many different areas of expertise. Every person in every job doesn't need to be certified. There should be one course and one examination for everyone who needs to be certified, and for one very logical reason. The business should have everyone on the same page of the hymnal, working toward the same objective.

Ad managers need to understand the creative team. The creative team needs to understand account managers and clients. Everyone needs to see the big picture and understand the other players. Some people need to be certified, others don't.

To be certified	No certification
Advertising managers & directors	Production mgrs.
Marketing managers & directors	Media planners
Agency top management	Advertiser mgmt.
Account planners	Graphic designers
Account executives & managers	
Account supervisors	
Creative directors	
Copywriters	
Art directors	
Advertising consultants	

On completion of the test, a person should receive a certificate and the right to call themselves something appropriate, like a Certified Advertising Practitioner.

Working with the American Association of Advertising Agencies, Association of National Advertisers, American Advertising Federation, American Marketing Association and local advertising organizations, this certification should be something of worth.

Chapter 12

HOW THE PROBLEMS WORK TOGETHER

How The Problems Reinforce Each Other

Having examined the 10 problems, let's take a quick overview of how they work together to cause ineffectiveness and waste money.

1. The vast majority of the people on both the client and agency sides of the business have had **little or no training** in what makes advertising effective. They learn from more experienced practitioners, who weren't trained either, and who pass on flawed philosophies.

2. Add the fact that there are **no commonly accepted standards** of what constitutes effective advertising, and you have an industry that doesn't know what its objective is or how to reach it.

3. To fill this void, we commonly use two evaluative criteria to define good advertising: Sales, or the number of awards won by the creative work. **Neither is a reliable measure of advertising effectiveness**, so the result is that we continue to produce ineffective work.

4. Since we know neither how to define nor how to measure advertising effectiveness, **we misuse and abuse research techniques.** We are consumed with fear that we will be blamed for ineffectiveness. This leads to poor decisions on creative work.

5. **The award shows have vague evaluative criteria, turning them largely into beauty contests.** They tend to reward art and advertainment while ignoring effectiveness.

6. Both agency and client types **look to the award show winners for a definition of good creative work.** This ensures the continued **creation of ineffective ads.**

In summary, most people in the advertising industry:

- haven't had proper training
- don't really understand what their job is
- don't know what evaluative criteria to use
- don't know how to measure effectiveness
- would rather be artistic than persuasive
- don't know how the approval process should work

The bottom line is that they have worked together to bring the industry to the point where advertising is largely ineffective.

Advertising Is in a Downward Spiral

Look at your TV, listen to your radio, read your magazines. The conclusion is inescapable. A lot of American advertisers have lost faith in their products and/or in their ad agencies' ability to craft strong, persuasive, product-focused advertising.

Read the last sentence again. It should make the hair on your neck stand up. What these people view as a reasonable approach in the face of overwhelming odds is, in fact, a gesture of surrender.

This is a self-fulfilling prophecy that will lead to ever lower expectations until, at the low point, these advertisers will throw up their hands in frustration and cry out in angst, "Advertising doesn't work for us any more."

I say to them, "You haven't been doing advertising for a long time. You gave up on it because you were afraid to attack the problems inherent in mass communication. You decided to become entertainers and failed, because the public knew it was still advertising. So now your ads sit flaccidly in the middle of nowhere, neither entertaining nor informative."

"Advertainment, by its very nature, has nothing to offer. You forgot that advertising has an important business communication function. You tried desperately to make advertising palatable because you were afraid your ads would make people mad. In so doing, you fell into a communication black hole, where no enlightenment is given off."

Chapter 13

WHERE TO GO FROM HERE

Advertisers Are the Key

The fastest, perhaps the only way to get the advertising industry on the effectiveness bandwagon is for advertisers to demand it. This means the first task is to educate advertisers about the situation, encouraging them to use specific evaluative criteria that will more accurately assess the likelihood that their advertising will be effective.

If advertisers tell their agencies they want effective advertising above all, and work with the same evaluative criteria, the agencies will do their best to give it to them. It won't come without some initial grumbling from the creative cave, but it definitely will come.

The good news is that advertisers are eager to have effective advertising. The bad news is that they either think they are getting it now or they have lowered their expectations of what advertising can do to a point where they will accept almost anything.

Inside Advertising Agencies

To shift the advertising agency mindset from award-winning advertainment to effective advertising, you have to start at the top, with agency management. This is where agency philosophy is determined, and concern for client success is greatest.

Once top management sees the wisdom of doing effective advertising, the effectiveness philosophy and appropriate evaluative criteria will be given to account managers, who will welcome it because it gives structure and direction to the creative process.

What Will the Creatives Think?

With some trepidation, management will also introduce the creative department to effectiveness advertising. The idea of making the transition from advertainment to effective advertising may, to the over-reactors, seem like an attempt to stifle their creativity and force them to do dull, boring work.

It conjures up visions of a creative team fettered in handcuffs and leg irons, sitting in a stultifying empty gray room. They write a word, consult an endless list of approved words and ideas, erase the word and once again scan the list with lifeless eyes, hoping to find something that will pass muster as the sand cascades through the hourglass and the deadline nears.

That's not at all what I'm suggesting. All I'm saying is that there are certain standards for effective marketing communication that should guide creative efforts. Effective advertising benefits everyone. There's no reason not to like it.

Don't be surprised if the creatives scoff for a while, until they realize it isn't anti-creative, it's just differently-creative. Most importantly, they will find there is nothing to prevent effective advertising from being clever and stunning and hilarious and award-winning. This discovery will enable creatives to be at peace with the idea.

Creatives Will Benefit

The effectiveness approach will have two major benefits to the creative team. The first benefit is they will have their task clearly defined. This may not sound like a big deal, but one of the toughest things a creative team faces is a vague or changing definition of what the advertising is supposed to do, and the limiting factors which need to be considered.

The second benefit of effectiveness-based advertising is that it makes the approval process easier and faster because everyone is playing by the same rules. It will also make it possible for everyone involved to be intelligent and consistent in their analysis.

The client can't get away with making cryptic, valueless pronouncements like, "It just doesn't speak to me" or "I was thinking of something a little punchier." Evaluative criteria force clients to deal with specific issues in specific terms.

The result will be more effective creative, achieved more quickly and with no relationship-threatening disagreements over how to define good creative.

The Research Folks Can Help Too

An excellent way to get both advertisers and agencies thinking effectiveness is to encourage research firms to have an effectiveness mindset. They are impartial third parties. Their credibility will make it easier for both sides to internalize this new approach to creative development.

Reaching this audience with the effectiveness message and the specific evaluative criteria is important. These criteria will be a big help to research firms who now have no consistent criteria against which to measure advertising effectiveness.

Proper and consistent evaluative criteria will make the measurement of advertising effectiveness easier to conduct and more accurate, because the evaluative criteria will be consistent over time, and useful in all creative applications and situations.

What About the Award Shows?

It's important that the creators of effective advertising get the recognition they deserve. The push for effectiveness-based advertising would be further accelerated by new award shows based on effectiveness evaluative criteria.

That's why I started The Zephyr Awards, an annual advertising creative competition in which judging is done using the effectiveness-based criteria recommended in this book. For more information on The Zephyr Awards, check out our web site at www.zephyrawards.com.

What We Can Do to Get Effective Advertising

1. Find some leaders in this fragmented industry who are willing to take on the task of leading the industry out of the advertainment age and into the effectiveness age.

2. Encourage everyone in the business to use common criteria in creating, evaluating and approving advertising.

3. Establish professional certification standards to improve the intellectual and professional capabilities of practitioners.

4. Require periodic training and professional development.

5. Encourage advertisers to demand work from their agencies using effectiveness-based evaluative criteria.

6. Encourage award shows to use these evaluative criteria in judging their contests.

Who Will Lead the Charge?

At some point, it will be helpful to identify the industry leaders who can orchestrate this difficult process. Who is qualified, credible, representative and powerful enough to represent this diverse industry?

The moguls who own the media powerhouses? Creative directors who have won lots of creative awards? The American Association of Advertising Agencies? Presidents of large agencies? Marketing and advertising managers from large clients?

Perhaps the biggest question is this: Who would be willing to suggest that the industry has lost its way? Who would be bold enough to state that the industry needs to change the way it does business? Who would be strong enough to ask creatives to accept a new definition of good creative, and suggest guidelines that creatives would perceive as limitations on their creativity?

You Can Do Something

You can be part of the solution. You can help the advertising industry get back on track. Periodically remind yourself and others that the job of advertising is to change minds by changing knowledge, beliefs and attitudes. Use the evaluative criteria from this book and encourage as well as challenge others to do so.

You'll encounter resistance to using these criteria, but you have the two ultimate weapons on your side – logic and common sense. Expect some people to argue with these criteria and the concept of effective advertising. They'll argue, but they can't win.

Making decisions based on "feel" is not as smart as making decisions based on objectives, common sense and logic.

PART II

THE SOLUTIONS

Chapter 14

THE FIFTEEN SECRETS OF EXTREMELY PERSUASIVE ADVERTISING

Here are fifteen secrets that will dramatically increase the likelihood that your advertising will be effective. I would call them rules, but in advertising, some of the most effective work breaks rules.

An ad does not need to rank high on all the factors to be an acceptable ad, but the more of these criteria it meets, the greater its persuasive power.

Remember the Job of Advertising

The objective of your advertising should be to help change minds and increase the likelihood of a purchase by changing three things – knowledge, beliefs and attitudes.

Changes in knowledge lead to changes in beliefs, which lead to attitude changes, which lead to behavior changes. There are many places along this continuum where you can target your advertising. Selecting the right place is an important decision.

Have a Good Reason

When you use these criteria to guide the development of your advertising, use common sense and keep an open mind.

Should you look at every piece of advertising with your checklist in hand? YES. Should you evaluate your ad on every one of the 15 factors? YES. Does the advertising have to meet all 15 guidelines to be a good ad? NO.

If an ad doesn't meet a "requirement," that's OK, as long as you have considered that option and have a valid reason for selecting a different approach.

Take the Job Seriously

Don't ever underestimate the difficulty of creating an ad that will actually persuade someone. Getting people to change their minds and habits is extremely difficult.

If you have any illusions that it's easy to produce advertising that works, consider these facts about the people you're trying to reach:

- They don't care about your advertising
- They don't want to see or hear it.
- They don't find your advertising all that entertaining.
- They won't work to understand your advertising.
- They probably won't remember your message.
- What they need from you is information about your product.

You have to tell people what you have for them, and give them specific and credible reasons to believe what you say. You have to address the criteria that people use to make their decisions. Find out what the important decision points are and create ads aimed at those points.

Give both practical and emotional information, along with specifics they can use in their decision process. Leave the generalities and meaningless fluff on the cutting room floor.

Approve Ads with Evaluative Criteria in Hand

Advertising should be neither created nor approved because of how it looks, how funny it is, how clever it is or how many awards it is likely to win. Advertising is business communication, not entertainment.

Bring your evaluative criteria worksheet with you to any meeting where advertising creative is being planned, reviewed or approved. It will make it easier to make smart decisions, and you won't overlook anything.

The worksheet shown on pages 164-165 is a good one to use as is, or you can adapt it to your particular needs.

Secret #1. Put messaging before entertaining.

You are a business communicator. You are not an entertainer. Your job is to persuade people to change their minds, so don't spend too much time being cute, clever, subtle or funny, leaving too little time for the message.

Not all humorous, clever or cute advertising is ineffective. These devices can contribute greatly to the persuasive power of an advertisement that delivers a simple and pertinent message, including a Big Promise and specific reasons to believe it.

Creative work that spends so much time entertaining that there isn't time to promote the product is not effective. Advertising that delivers a clear, strong message with humor, riveting visuals and must-read writing is generally very effective.

Toyota: Great Cars, Great Advertising

I admit that I am a big fan of Toyota. I own two of the them, and my next car will be a Toyota. I'm also big fan of Toyota's intelligent advertising.

The Toyota truck ad on the next page is an excellent example of how to use humor, and it includes a wonderful combination of emotional and factual information.

Demonstration is the most powerful thing you can do in advertising. The photo is a powerful demonstration. The headline is a clever appeal to the audience machismo.

The copy at the bottom is brief and fact filled. The ad is filled with testosterone, but in a wonderfully understated way. Part of a fine, consistent campaign.

129

Secret #2. Make a Big Promise and give reasons to believe it.

Big Promise

A Big Promise is the most important personal benefit a product offers to customers. It answers the question, "What is in it for me?" The Big Promise can be expressed in many ways.

Over the years, different words, visuals and demonstrations will be used to make the Big Promise, but the promise should be consistent over time.

A Big Promise is not synonymous with a tag line, although a great tag line often contains the Big Promise. A Big Promise is not a description of the product. If you're selling ice cream, "17% butterfat" is not a Big Promise. Rich, creamy taste is.

A Big Promise should not be general or vague. Make it as specific as you can and still cover the varying needs, wants and situations of your target audience. If you do nothing else in your advertising, make it unmistakably clear what your product offers the buyer.

Big Promise Examples

Look younger than your actual age.

People will look up to you.

You'll lose weight.

You'll have more money.

Your wife will love you.

Reasons to Believe the Big Promise

A Big Promise is important, but don't forget to support your claim. An ad must give people compelling reasons why they should believe the promise and believe that the product is right for them.

This can involve both factual and emotional information, preferably both. It's better to give one or two major reasons, rather than a whole list. Reasons should be as specific as possible.

Creatives often use as little copy as possible, thinking that people won't read a lot of copy. They think that copy is ugly and detracts from the beauty of the ad. Advertising can be attractive and effective at the same time. It just requires the same dedication to excellence that any ad deserves.

Just because long copy "sells more" than short copy doesn't mean you should write a lot. Use as few words as possible to get your point across clearly, completely and powerfully.

RoC Knows How to Make a Big Promise

The RoC ad on the following page does an outstanding job of making a strong Big Promise and giving strong, succinct reasons to believe it. What a great Big Promise, and it's delivered powerfully by the visual, headline and "I'm 43" personal note. The small amount of body copy gives strong support for the promise. This ad rocs. Sorry, I couldn't resist.

Secret #3. Use a Big Idea to deliver your Big Promise.

Ads are more powerful when based on a big creative idea. Good Big Ideas almost always have something to do with the Big Promise and the product. Some memorable Big Ideas include:

- **Wendy's** "Where's the Beef?" campaign, which used a feisty little old lady (Clara Peller) to call attention to the fact that you could actually see the beef on Wendy's hamburgers. You could see it because the patty was square, not because the patty was bigger, but the idea worked anyway.

- **Motel 6** has used for years the good-old-boy voice of Tom Bodett to deliver the line, "And we'll leave the light on for you" to position the chain as friendly and welcoming.

- **MasterCard** has consistently made the point that you can use its card for anything by telling you that some things are priceless, but "for everything else, there's MasterCard."

- **Quaker Oats** promoted its Life breakfast cereal with the help of hard-to-please "Mikey" and the idea that if he liked it, it must be really, really good.

Plays on words and double entendre are not Big Ideas. Putting something about elections in your ads prior to national elections is not a Big Idea. Having your car zooming around a digitally produced countryside, just like every other car manufacturer, is not a Big Idea.

Boo on Borrowed Interest

Using borrowed interest is often not a Big Idea. In fact, it's a terrible idea when you spend more time with the borrowed interest than you do with the message it's supposed to help convey.

Borrowed interest is something you bring into your advertising to try to make it more interesting. Some people think of it as a Big Idea, but it is often used to cover up the lack of a Big Idea.

You see a lot of borrowed interest in TV commercials. Fake game shows and fake news shows are two frequently used pieces of borrowed interest. A celebrity spokesperson is a type of borrowed interest. If you get the right person, it can work better than most borrowed interest.

The danger of using borrowed interest is that it often takes up so much time or space that there isn't enough time to give the message. It's a real problem if you remember the borrowed interest but not the message.

Be bold, unusual, innovative and unique with your borrowed interest, but make the product the hero. One Big Idea used consistently over time will be much more effective than a string of little ideas disguised with borrowed interest.

Secret #4. Create Big Idea campaigns, not small idea "Onezies."

Logic tells you that consistency of message over time is critical to all advertisers. It's important that you are consistent with all factors. Make the same Big Promise, with the same supporting messages, using the same creative Big Idea, in the same general format.

Use an advertising campaign for as long as you can. Advertisers and agencies get tired of their advertising long before the target audience does. Don't let boredom be the impetus for changing the advertising program. A little variation within a lot of consistency should be your goal.

Your audience will remember your name and your main message better if you create a series of similar ads, rather than a string of onezie ads that don't look or sound alike.

If you produce onezies, your audience has to start the familiarization and remembering process anew every time. This makes it easier to forget prior advertising messages, and harder for your audience to store your current or prior messages in long-term memory.

Secret #5. Give your product or company a personality.

This can be in the form of a spokesperson, such as an owner, president, employee, customer or paid presenter. It can also be a visual cue, like a cartoon character or animal, or an auditory cue such as a voice, tone of voice or piece of music (e.g. United Airlines using Gershwin's Rhapsody in Blue).

The purpose of "personality" is to help people remember your name and message, and put the two together. Personality is not the message of the ad, it is how the message is delivered, how your points are made more powerfully and memorably.

Look at how the Aflac duck and Energizer Bunny have been used with great success over the years. Or the Marlboro Man, one of the world's best known ad personalities. I don't think he ever spoke a word, but his persona lent a machismo to Marlboro cigarettes.

People relate to other people much more readily than they relate to things. Don't just show the car, show people enjoying the car. Don't just show a beautiful sunset, show a couple holding hands looking at it.

With the caveat that product personality is not necessarily directly related to advertising effectiveness, here are some examples of personality:

- **New York Life** uses Snoopy and his buddy Woodstock to inject light humor into life insurance.

- **Budweiser** has used the Clydesdales and frogs as continuing visual cues to engender positive feelings for the brand.

- **Wendy's** used its wonderful, personable founder, the late Dave Thomas, to give a credible quality and caring feel to customers.

- **Timex** used John Cameron Swayze, prominent newsman of the day, to give legitimacy to their powerful "It takes a licking and keeps on ticking" claim.

- **Allstate Insurance** has been consistent in making people feel protected by saying, "You're in good hands with Allstate."

- **Hamms Beer** for decades used a cartoon bear and a musical jingle "From the land of sky blue waters..." to achieve memorability.

- **United Parcel Service** turned its bland brown corporate color into a positive with the simple positioning line, "What can brown do for you?"

Secret #6. Make an emotional connection with your audience.

Every decision has an emotional component. The biggest decisions in your life -- spouse, house, auto, college, career, friends and vacations – are all greatly affected by emotions.

With all the clutter and competition for attention, advertising has to have a lot of emotional oomph to cut through the background noise.

It isn't enough that an ad be okay, acceptable, or even good. Every ad you do has to be superior to what your competitors and other advertisers are doing. If it isn't, it's not going to work as hard as it should.

When you look at the piece of advertising, ask yourself, "Does this ad stir a strong feeling in me?" Anger, sadness, happiness, admiration, patriotism – whatever? What in the advertising causes the feeling?

Your job isn't to create a good, solid ad. Your job is to make your target audience tingly, to strike an emotional chord that will get them thinking in a positive, emotional way about your product.

Secret #7. Require powerful, colorful, persuasive writing.

Most advertising writing is pretty unimpressive, even boring. Generalities, advertising speak, clichés, stuff you've read and heard a thousand times, and don't want to see again.

Writing doesn't have to be flowery or inspiring to be persuasive. If the copy reads easily and is full of information, that's all you need to change people's minds. There are a few keys to effective copywriting:

A. Be specific.

Generalities are unpersuasive. Specifics give people the facts, figures and details they require to make a decision. Here are some sentences from the body copy of actual print ads. Which of these is more likely to change knowledge, beliefs and attitudes?

- "Nothing helps you improve your perspective on the day quite like the ability to do things a little better, a little faster, and a little more beautifully."

- "Whether you're already transitioning into retirement or the day is still a few years away, we're here to help you switch gears."

- "With second-row seats that you can fold down, split or remove, the (SUV name) is ready for anything. And thanks to standard features like Vehicle Stability Control plus Traction Control and an Anti-lock Brake System, wherever you go, we'll help get you there safely, which is always much more enjoyable."

- "People look to a number of sources to help them make their health care choices. Some are better than others. At (company name), we provide our members with the information they need to make better decisions."

My money would be on the third one, which has specific information that I could use to make a smarter decision.

B. <u>Use power words.</u>

Use words you don't hear every day, but that people will understand. Adverbs and adjectives are weak. Verbs are powerful. It's advertising, not a novel, but strive diligently to make ad copy as interesting as the books we read for pleasure. Don't settle for the expected, superficial writing that populates so much of today's advertising. You can do better.

C. <u>Write like people talk.</u>

Advertising is a stand-in for personal selling. As such, it should try to emulate the person-to-person experience as much as possible. People don't usually talk in long sentences.

The reason this kind of writing is so inviting to read or listen to, and so persuasive, is that you can feel the personality in the writing.

Secret #8. Demonstrate.

A powerful demonstration of the most important product benefit is the most effective advertising approach. You can take that to the bank.

Timex is an old, but still great example. Its campaign showed over and over how damage-resistant and long-lasting its watches were.

Timex hasn't been on TV for decades, yet young people know their famous tag line and their TV spots. Why do the kiddies know about them? Their elders told them about the spots. Now that's the power of demonstration.

Another example of a powerful demonstration also comes from the past. Rolls Royce did some TV advertising many years ago. A questionable strategy for a product with a tiny target audience, but that's not the point. One Rolls Royce spot was one of the best demonstrations I have ever seen.

The commercial was simple. A well-dressed Englishman exited an office building and got into a Rolls Royce. The door closed with a solid, muffled thud and the car accelerated away down the street. The commercial cut to the car going sixty miles an hour on a freeway. You saw the man sitting in the back seat, the chauffeur, and close-ups of the speedometer and the car's clock. No music, no dialogue, virtually no sound.

Toward the end of the spot, a deep male voice with a distinguished English accent said in measured tones, "At sixty miles per hour, the loudest sound in a Rolls Royce is the clock."

In automobiles, we equate a quiet ride with quality. What more did they need to say? Demonstrations are simple and powerful, and are easier to believe and remember than lots of copy or statistics.

Yet another example of an outstanding demonstration comes from the past, 1980-81 to be exact. The product was Schlitz beer, which in the mid 70's was the number two brewery in the country. Schlitz tried to lower costs by changing some of its brewing processes, which resulted in quality problems and plummeting sales.

Schlitz eventually fixed their product problems, but their market share had slipped alarmingly, and they felt something bold had to be done in an attempt to regain their former stature in the industry.

Schlitz began a unique series of TV commercials which featured live blind taste tests. The commercials ran during half time of televised professional football games.

One hundred beer drinkers who claimed to be loyal drinkers of a competitive brand drank (off-camera, of course) the competitive brand and Schlitz from unmarked containers. A referee blew his whistle and the men indicated electronically which of the beers they liked better.

This may seem like a dangerous and panicky move, but Schlitz was smart. They knew that a lot of beer drinkers can't tell the difference among the major brands in blind tastings. Sure enough, 38-50 % of the drinkers chose Schlitz instead of the brand they said was their favorite.

Unfortunately, this is not a success story. The negative publicity about the production quality had been a death blow to Schlitz, one that even innovative and imaginative advertising couldn't repair, and Schlitz eventually passed from the scene.

Though it happened over twenty-five years ago, I included this story here for three reasons:

1. It shows the power of a well-conceived demonstration.
2. It demonstrates the value of having a thorough knowledge of your audience.
3. There aren't many good demonstrations in today's advertising, so you have to go back a few years to get some goodies.

Demonstration on Radio

There is a strong tendency to talk too much in radio. This bores the poor listeners and wastes the client's money. Because we are a visually-oriented society, a lot of copywriters don't use in their radio commercials the most powerful type of ad – demonstration.

It's a lot easier than you think to demonstrate on radio. We have five senses – taste, feel, smell, hearing and sight. We are used to demonstrations on TV where sight is the primary or only sense involved.

Remember, the strength of radio is that you can engage the listener's imagination and get them to visualize their own version of your commercial, getting them very involved in the process.

When you work on a radio commercial, use one or more of the other four senses. You'll find it's easier to make an unusual, intriguing and effective ad.

Secret #9 Don't mention the competition.

There has long been disagreement within the advertising community over whether comparisons with a competitor's product are wise. I think mentioning a competitor's product is rarely smart. It doesn't matter whether you are the category leader or the smallest company in the category.

Why Nobody Should Compare

If you mention or make obvious reference to any other brand in your category, three things happen, none of them good for you.

First, you are giving your competitor free advertising. Granted, you are only giving product visibility and name awareness, but they are very important. Why would you want to give any competitor free time or space for which you paid?

Second, whenever a lower ranking brand and a higher ranking brand are mentioned in the same commercial, there is natural confusion about who is the sponsor. This can happen when people aren't paying much attention, which is common.

When there is uncertainty about the sponsor's name, people will usually attribute the ad to the better known brand.

Third, by mentioning two or more product names, your advertising loses much of its focus and clarity. People don't pay nearly as much attention to advertising as advertisers would like, and misunderstandings are rampant. In addition to giving away free advertising, you're also weakening your own message and confusing your audience.

Whoever you are, you're better off talking about how good your product is, not how lacking the other guy's is. Negative advertising may work in politics, but that's because it's impossible to know a politician's stances on all the issues and what they're really thinking.

Another reason is that by taking on the competition by name, you may implicitly reinforce perceptions of the competitor(s) as the category leader(s). Saying "we're as good as BMW" probably does more to reinforce BMW's leadership than it does to bolster the challenger.

The Exception to the Rule

You can use competitors' names in one situation. If you are not the category sales leader, but you are the category leader on an important factor, listing you and the major competitors in print ads can be a good thing.

This only works if the factor is important to buyers and you are clearly superior to everyone else in the category. It has to be done in print format so the audience has time to study the statistics. A brief mention on radio or TV isn't enough to establish the facts.

A Big Waste of Money

When one company's advertising refers to a close competitor, it is bad. When the competitor then produces an ad that "answers" the first company's ad, giving free exposure back to the first company, it is worse.

During the 2004 Presidential election, one of the top beer makers did a TV spot that said their beer was the President of beers. The industry leader, knowing that the first firm is owned by a Canadian company, answered with an ad that cleverly made the point that the first company's beer can never be President, since you have to be born in America to be eligible for the Presidency.

Clever and entertaining? For sure. Effective advertising for either company? Not at all. I was surprised twice by this exchange. Initially, I was shocked that a lagging competitor would give the industry leader free air time. I was then astonished when the industry leader lowered itself by producing a "onezie" answer ad, which gave visibility and credibility to the lower-ranking competitor.

I learned two things from this incident. First, beer sales must be good if these two biggies have enough money to waste on silly and ineffective advertising like this. Second, even the big boys can use a course in effective advertising.

Secret #10. Don't rely on special effects, sex, animals or kids.

Special Effects

Creative people like to use special effects. With today's technology, there is almost nothing they can't do to make ads entertaining. The danger, however, is that you end up with advertising that is all about the effects, overwhelming any message the advertiser is trying to deliver, and making the advertising a waste of money.

Special effects shouldn't be used to dramatize or demonstrate a Big Promise. Simplicity is much to be desired in advertising. When you pummel viewers with special effects, they may end up remembering only the visuals, and nothing about the message.

Sex

You've heard the saying, "Sex sells." But does it? The obvious question is, "Does sex sell?" The real question is, "Is it sexy images that sell, or is it the promise that a product can make us more attractive to the opposite sex that convinces us to buy?"

For certain products, a beautiful woman or a sculpted man in an ad can help you visualize the Big Promise, making the ad more persuasive. In these cases, the advertisers are using the person's presence to say to the audience, "If you buy our product, your chances of attracting a woman or men like this will increase." This is a legitimate use of the promise of sex to sell.

Similarly, an attractive man or woman can be a legitimate demonstration for a product such as exercise equipment, diet plans or health clubs.

On the other hand, use of a good-looking person to sell a product which has nothing to do with sexual attractiveness is going to take focus away from the main message, making the ad less effective. In effect, the advertiser is saying they can't come up with a strong Big Promise, and are simply playing the sex card to gain your attention.

Kids and Kittens

Then there are kids and animals. Cute, cuddly, lovable. Advertisers have been using kids and animals for decades to bring warmth and positive emotions to their ads.

The commonly held belief is that an ad is guaranteed to be good if it has them. The truth is that some are effective and some are not. There is nothing inherently bad with using kids or pets. The danger is that their use is so prominent as to drown out the Big Promise and reasons to believe the promise.

Secret #11. If you have a tag line, make it memorable.

Most clients and agencies assume that a tag line is an important part of a marketing program. Actually, most tag lines are useless. Nobody is as interested in an advertiser's tag line as the advertiser.

Think about it. In, if you haven't made your point in the first twenty-seven seconds of your TV spot, how much value does a two-second tag line have? If you don't make your case in the other seventy-nine square inches of your full page magazine ad, what good is that one square inch dedicated to the tag line?

It takes a long time for a few words to become memorable. Patience and persistence are absolutely necessary in establishing a valuable and memorable tag line.

See for yourself what works and what doesn't. Take the Tag Line Test. Write down the company's name associated with each tag line listed on page 151. It's best not to write in the book, so you can have others take the test. Answers are on the back of that page.

Doing it Right

In many instances, a well crafted tag line can increase the memorability of the company or product. A tag line is best used to repeat and reinforce the Big Promise. The next best thing is to connect the sponsor name with the Big Promise.

Most tag lines are so general that most companies in the world could use them. If a person can't make a strong connection between the tag line and the company, the line is no good. It's no wonder research shows that most tag lines aren't associated with the correct company.

The first requirement for an effective tag line is to include the company or product name and the Big Promise. The second, and equally crucial requirement, is that it be used consistently for years, even decades.

Tag Line Test

Write in the company for each tag line.
(Answers on reverse side)

1. Invent
2. _____ Country
3. When you care enough to send the very best
4. Wake up and drive
5. We move the world
6. Get the feeling
7. Imagination at work
8. Win
9. You've got questions. We've got answers
10. Grab life by the horns
11. Make every mile count
12. The Diamond Store
13. Like a good neighbor, _____ is there.
14. Don't just travel. Travel Right.
15. It's everywhere you want to be
16. The relief goes on
17. You're in good hands
18. It takes a licking and keeps on ticking
19. There are some things money can't buy, for everying else, there's _____
20. Make it your own
21. Welcome to the state of independence
22. Defining Beauty
23. The passionate pursuit of perfection
24. Dermatologist recommended
25. The signature of American style
26. The world's best tasting vodka
27. For life
28. Discover nature's secret for beautifully smooth skin
29. The new look of comfort
30. You'll see. We're better.

Tag Line Test Answers

1. Hewlett Packard
2. Marlboro Cigarettes or Ford
3. Hallmark
4. Mitsubishi
5. DHL
6. Toyota
7. General Electric
8. Hyundai
9. Radio Shack
10. Dodge
11. Kia
12. Zales
13. State Farm Insurance
14. Expedia.com
15. Visa
16. Allegra (allergy)
17. Allstate Insurance
18. Timex
19. Mastercard
20. Saks Fifth Avenue
21. Saab
22. Estee Lauder
23. Lexus
24. Neutrogena
25. Lord & Taylor
26. Grey Goose
27. Volvo
28. Aveeno
29. La Z Boy
30. Lens crafters

Don't feel bad if you didn't get very many. A score of 15 or above is very good.

Secret #12. Write radio right.

Writing an effective radio commercial is the most difficult thing in advertising. Most of the spots you hear have been written by either a salesperson from the radio station who has never had a minute of creative training, or an agency copywriter who drew the short straw.

Radio is tough to write because it lacks visuals. That scares a lot of writers because we all think visually. Sight is a stronger sense than hearing, so a good picture can communicate more quickly and with greater accuracy than a lot of words.

Not only is it tougher to write radio, it is more enjoyable and easier to write TV because it is easier to demonstrate. With the technology available today, if someone can imagine it, you can show it.

This is about as much as most people think about radio. They never even consider that radio has something no other medium has - the ability to get listeners to help make the commercial. Not only make it, but tailor it to their own personality and situation.

Imagination Is the Key

What is this magic power? Imagination. The more you can get your audience involved in your advertising, rather than just observing it, the more likely you are to change their minds. One way to involve someone is to get them to imagine themselves as the star of the show.

Given the right suggestions, information and situations, listeners will produce a version of the commercial that relates directly to them. For example, if you're writing a TV spot for a nice restaurant that involves showing food, you have to choose a specific menu item. You have to try to show something that will appeal to as many people as possible. Let's say you choose a filet mignon steak. It will look great, but that selection has decreased the strength and interest of the commercial for all the people who don't like filet mignon.

Now you're writing a radio spot for the same restaurant. If you're smart, you can provide opportunities for listeners to customize the commercial for themselves. Instead of saying filet mignon, you say, "The waiter has just placed your favorite special occasion food in front of you. You can't wait for that first bite." You have invited listeners to come up with their favorite. You have challenged them to select a dish, and in so doing, have involved them in the commercial.

When you involve someone in advertising to the point that they use their imagination to construct a spot that is specific to them, you are well on your way to writing an effective commercial.

If you're going to spend money on radio, you might as well make it count. Don't treat radio as TV's poor relative. Don't assume you can't get a memorable radio commercial or campaign written. Pay the same amount of attention to radio as you do to TV.

Secret #13. Be bold, be different

You can't bore people into changing their minds. That's why you should demand more from your advertising than that it just meet certain requirements and contain the required information.

There is no shortage of expected, bland, unremarkable advertising. It's not that hard to be bold and different, but it does require a client willing to take intelligent chances.

Don't be different just to be different. Be unusual so that people will like looking at it, so they will spend time with it, and be more likely to remember it. Sometimes it's a visual thing, sometimes it's the copy, ideally, it's both.

When you're going for bold and different, remember that this is not a substitute for a strong product message. People won't buy your product because you do wacky commercials. They'll buy your product because the wacky commercials delivered a strong Big Promise in a way that forged an emotional connection with the audience.

Secret #14. Make your print ads easy on the eyes.

Your ad has to fight its way through a lot of clutter to make a lasting impression. People won't work hard to try to understand what you ad is trying to tell them, so take heed.

Make Your Big Promise Obvious

You don't make points with your audience by using blind headlines or clever plays on words. You make points by telling them simply and strongly what you have for them.

Make it Easy to Read

Your ad should follow the way we are taught to read – from top to bottom, from left to right, which combine to give us an upper-left to lower-right flow of our eyes.

Use Size to Indicate Importance

Bigger is better in our society. Whether editorial or advertising, headlines are big and the main visual is big. People expect to see certain things. Don't make it harder for them to get your message, make it easier.

Secret #15. Tell your TV story with pictures.

Your audience uses two senses to take in a TV commercial – sight and hearing. Remember that people cannot look and listen with the same intensity. We are a visual society and visuals are almost always more attention-getting than sounds.

Since people will generally pay more attention to what you show than what you say, make sure your Big Promise and key message can be seen on screen. If they can also be heard in the dialogue or voice-over, that's even better.

A common mistake in making television commercials is to have important information and key messages given by voice-over while the visuals are showing a different story. This may seem to be a clever presentation, but the truth is that the messages aren't getting across. People are paying more intention to the visuals, and aren't really hearing what's being said off camera.

Chapter 15

A CREATIVE PHILOSOPHY

I have used the term "evaluative criteria" throughout this book. The criteria you use to create, evaluate and approve advertising can also be called your creative philosophy.

If someone were to ask you, "What is your creative philosophy," what would you say? Stumped? You're not alone. Few people in the advertising industry have a written philosophy about the business and what makes "great creative.".

My creative philosophy is embodied in a set of evaluative criteria I developed called S.T.E.P., an acronym for Strategies & Tactics for Effective Persuasion. The S.T.E.P. worksheet is shown on page 173. The actual worksheet fits on one side of an 8 1/2" x 11" sheet for ease of use.

It gives you a consistent idea of what you are doing. It is a tool to help you focus on issues that will result in more persuasive, more effective communication. With S.T.E.P. as your guide, there's no guessing or making decisions by the seat of your pants.

S.T.E.P. Is a Creative Philosophy

Many decisions have to be made in the course of creating an ad. These decisions are made by the copywriter, art director, creative director, account manager and one or more people at the client. If you have a say in the creation or approval of advertising, you definitely should have a creative philosophy.

An example of a creative philosophy comes from one of the industry's heroes, William Bernbach, quoted in *Bill Bernbach*. "The truth isn't the truth until people believe you, and they can't believe you if they don't know what you're saying, and they can't know what you're saying if they don't listen to you, and they won't listen to you if you're not interesting, and you won't be interesting unless you say things imaginatively, originally, freshly."

One reason the industry is in deep trouble is that people make suggestions and decisions based on a loose collection of experiences, perceptions, beliefs, attitudes, feelings and habits. A creative philosophy should go deeper than, "I like it," "It doesn't do anything for me," or "I think it will work."

S.T.E.P. Is for Everybody

S.T.E.P. is a simple creative philosophy everyone can readily embrace and easily use. It replaces the usual "I say/You say" approach to the creative process with a consistent direction, structure and focus.

Account managers should use S.T.E.P. at two points: 1) when they write up a creative brief to guide the creative team's efforts; and 2) when they review the recommended creative work with their clients. The creative team should use S.T.E.P. as they create the advertising, and the clients should use it when they review and approve ads.

If even one person makes decisions based on nothing more than personal opinions and preferences, the process is much harder, and the likelihood of getting ineffective advertising increases. A person who doesn't use S.T.E.P. can impede the entire process.

How It Works

S.T.E.P. allows you to conduct a complete and accurate assessment of one ad, or to help identify which of a number of alternative ads is most likely to be effective. It helps everyone involved to focus on the key factors associated with effective advertising.

Based on the assumption that the objective of advertising is to change knowledge, beliefs and attitudes, it provides as much specificity and direction as possible, while still fostering innovative thinking and unique creative solutions.

How to Use S.T.E.P.

It is best to begin by having everyone involved in the approval process look at the ads and fill out their S.T.E.P. form before any discussions take place. After everyone has done this, it's time to exchange ideas and come to a consensus.

S.T.E.P. is a common language which all the participants in the creative process can use in the planning, development, evaluation and approval of advertising for all media.

It is not a mathematical formula. It does not produce numerical scores. It does not tell creatives what appeals to make, how to write copy, what visuals to use, or how to put together the various parts into a complete piece of advertising.

It Doesn't Select the Winner

The numbers you put down on your S.T.E.P. worksheet are not grades. They are indications of how strong or weak you feel the ad currently is on each factor. The scores on the fifteen factors should not be added up for the purpose of selecting a winner.

That's right, these numbers should not be used to select the best ad. That is not the job of S.T.E.P. Analysis and assessment of advertising effectiveness is highly subjective. Don't use S.T.E.P. to provide statistics to support arguments for or against an ad.

It should be used to pinpoint the weak and strong parts of an ad, and to help determine when an ad is fit to be presented to the public.

S.T.E.P. also helps prevent an otherwise strong ad from getting dumped because it is weak on one factor. It is normal to find both good and bad parts in an ad.

Scoring

There are typically two rounds of scoring using S.T.E.P. Seldom is a piece of advertising so perfect right out of the box that it is approved without changes. Identifying and making changes that will improve an ad are normal and important parts of the creative process. Thus, you should expect two or more rounds of review.

The first round is to identify areas for improvement. When considering multiple ads, it is unwise to make any yea or nay decisions in the first session. Once improvements are made in the weak areas of all the ads under consideration, an ad which did quite poorly in the first round can become the best ad in the second round.

Completed worksheets are very helpful in keeping discussions focused. Multiple participants should come to a consensus on areas of desired improvement before giving direction to the creative team.

After revisions have been made, the revised creative work is presented, and the second round of reviewing is done. Participants should use the same sheet for both rounds, to easily note whether changes are improvements or only changes.

S.T.E.P.

Strategies & Tactics for Effective Persuasion

Big Promise:_____

> Circle a number. 5 is highest; 1 is lowest.
> Use the left set of numbers for original work, and the
> right set of numbers for subsequent revised work.

1. Does the ad put messaging before entertaining?
   5 4 3 2 1   5 4 3 2 1

2. Is there a Big Promise based on a major benefit
   and supported by emotional and/or factual
   information?
   5 4 3 2 1   5 4 3 2 1

3. Is a Big Idea used to deliver the Big Promise?
   5 4 3 2 1   5 4 3 2 1

4. Is this ad consistent with recent advertising in
   appearance, Big Promise, Big Idea and support?
   5 4 3 2 1   5 4 3 2 1

5. Is the product or company personality expressed?
   5 4 3 2 1   5 4 3 2 1

6. Does it make an emotional connection?
   5 4 3 2 1   5 4 3 2 1

7. Is the writing specific, interesting, easy to read?
   5 4 3 2 1   5 4 3 2 1

8. Is there a strong demonstration of the
   Big Promise?
   5 4 3 2 1   5 4 3 2 1

9. Does the ad refrain from using competitors' names?

5 4 3 2 1   5 4 3 2 1

10. Is the ad free of <u>distracting</u> special effects, sexual innuendo, double entendre, children, animals, etc.

5 4 3 2 1   5 4 3 2 1

11. Does tag line include name and a Big Promise?

5 4 3 2 1   5 4 3 2 1

12. If a radio spot, does it invite listener involvement?

5 4 3 2 1   5 4 3 2 1

13. If a print ad, is it easy to read and understand?
5 4 3 2 1   5 4 3 2 1

14. If a TV spot, does it tell the story with visuals?
5 4 3 2 1   5 4 3 2 1

15. Is the ad bold or unusual?
5 4 3 2 1   5 4 3 2 1

The results of the S.T.E.P. process are subjective, leaving a lot of room for opinion and disagreement. This is good. If a few people have varying opinions when reviewing advertising which millions will see, it's good to have a spirited discussion before coming to a consensus. In a business which has very few rules or even guidelines, airing differing ideas and positions is necessary and helpful.

Handling the Results

S.T.E.P. does not require that an ad receive high scores on all fifteen factors before it can be approved. An ad doesn't have to have high scores on every factor, or even several factors, to be effective. Great strength in a very few areas may be all that is necessary to be very effective.

All S.T.E.P. factors may not be applicable to every ad. If an ad doesn't deal with a factor, it isn't necessarily an indication of weakness. This is one reason why adding up the numbers to find the "best" ad is not the purpose.

Here's what to do after the first round:

1. Achieve consensus about the weaknesses and strengths.

2. Convey the results and suggestions to the creative team.

3. Give the team enough time to think and revise.

Here's what to do after the second round:

1. Determine if the identified weaknesses have been fixed, or that they cannot be fixed.

2. Put S.T.E.P. down and look at the revised ads.

3. Pretend you are in the target audience. Ask yourself which ad(s) would most likely change your mind.

4. Go with the ad you feel best delivers the Big Promise and gives reasons to believe it.

Be Reasonable

Don't let S.T.E.P. limit innovation or intelligent risk-taking. Ads are often effective because they break rules and defy convention. Ads which may at first seem inappropriate, hard to understand or bizarre sometimes turn out to be highly effective.

If the creative team feels strongly about these kinds of ads, open your mind really wide and listen to them. Remember, clients hire an agency in the hope the agency will produce superior work. Superior work is almost never safe and familiar.

Also, keep in mind that **you are in the business of changing minds, not entertaining them.** Demand that your advertising work hard for you.

It Makes Everyone's Life Easier

Everyone involved should be excited to have a tool like S.T.E.P. It lets everyone know, right from the beginning, what is expected from the advertising. It answers the question creatives sometimes ask clients or account managers, "What are you looking for here?"

It also answers the question clients and account managers sometimes ask the creative team, "What are you trying to say here?"

With S.T.E.P. it's all down in black and white. This means fewer surprises and disagreements over what advertising should do and how it should be done. The process is easier and less confrontational for everyone, and less expensive for the client.

S.T.E.P. gives specific feedback and direction to the creative team. This is very valuable. It's extremely frustrating for creatives to try to revise and improve work if clients and/or account managers give input based on vague generalizations and personal opinions such as "I don't know if that headline is strong enough," "I never have liked the word bereft," and "What if we did this instead?"

With S.T.E.P. you can be confident that the ad(s) you select will have a high likelihood of being an effective communication tool. Your decision will have been based on solid advertising knowledge and concepts, not whim or personal preferences.

Chapter 16

TO THE SMALL ADVERTISER

It's tough to define a small advertiser. It depends on the product, the geographic market served and how much the competition spends. Suffice it to say that you know who you are.

You're a small advertiser if the name on the door includes the words "Thai food." You're small if most of your competitors spend more on TV sitcom product placements than you do on your national TV schedule. You're small if your budget can't do a decent job in one medium when the enemy uses several media.

I've done creative work for a lot of small advertisers. They have always been my most rewarding challenges and my favorite clients. Because I have a soft spot in my heart for the little guy and the underdog, let me give you a few thoughts about how to maximize the impact of your ad budget.

Keep in mind that small advertisers should do the same things large advertisers do. The size of the playing field is different, but the things you have do to win are the same.

Success Secrets for the Small Advertiser

1. **Study.** Small doesn't mean stupid. When you're small, you have to be smarter. Learn from this book and keep it handy; it's your best friend in the ad business.

2. **Focus.** You're better off doing a good job using one medium, one station or one publication. If you use too many media, you'll end up being almost invisible in all of them.

3. **Persist.** Don't change your creative approach, your ads or your tag line like they were socks. Work hard to craft a strong Big Promise and deliver it consistently with a creative Big Idea. When you do change something in your ad program, have a good reason for it and something better to replace it.

4. **Resist.** Once you begin an advertising campaign, no matter how small or unsophisticated it may be, there are constant temptations to make a little change here, a little change there. A radio station may offer to write free commercials for you. A special section in a newspaper may seem a great way to target your audience. "Specials" almost always are better in concept than in reality. Say no.

5. **Demonstrate.** Don't try to mimic the clever, funny, expensive ads you see on TV. A demonstration is always your best shot.

6. **Connect.** Even if all you can afford is small print ads, make an emotional connection with your audience. Don't just show the product, show a person using it. Don't just talk product, talk people.

7. **Differentiate.** Success comes from a better product, not from advertising. Don't settle for "as good as." Have a unique product that offers more.

8. **Relate.** In any communication with your audience, act like you're talking face to face with one person. Don't write like you're talking to 100,000 faceless numbers. Write as if you were talking with a friend.

Chapter 17

AND IN CLOSING

- The advertising industry is unaware of its ten major problems:
    1. They have forgotten why advertising exists.
    2. They don't know the difference between clever and creative.
    3. The players have conflicting approaches and agendas.
    4. They aren't giving their audience what they want.
    5. There is no definition of great.
    6. They're not using research correctly.
    7. They're producing "onezies," not campaigns.
    8. The approval process is meaningless.
    9. The award show is advertising's drug of choice.
    10. They don't train their people.

- The fifteen secrets to extremely persuasive advertising are:
    1. Put messaging before entertaining.
    2. Make a Big Promise and give reasons to believe it.
    3. Use a Big Idea to deliver your Big Promise.
    4. Create Big Idea campaigns, not small idea onezies.
    5. Give your product or company a personality.
    6. Make an emotional connection with your audience.

7. Require powerful, colorful, persuasive writing.

8. Demonstrate (yes, even in radio).

9. Don't mention the competition.

10. Don't rely on special effects, sex, animals or kids.

11. If you have a tag line, make it memorable.

12. Write radio right – involve the listener's imagination.

13. Be bold, be different.

14. Make your print ads easy on the eyes.

15. Tell your TV story with pictures.

To ensure your advertising has the best chance to be effective, use S.T.E.P. (Strategies and Tactics for Effective Persuasion.). It gives better direction and focus to the creative development process.

It makes the review and approval process less contentious and more likely to result in effective advertising. It gives you confidence and the ability to produce effective advertising on an ongoing basis.

My Challenge to You

With S.T.E.P. and the other ideas you've seen in this book, you now have the capability and the opportunity to create more powerful, more persuasive and more productive advertising than you ever have. The possibilities are exciting. Take the bull, or whatever you have handy, by the horns and S.T.E.P. up to a new level of advertising excellence.

BIBLIOGRAPHY

This book is both an industry exposé and a how-to book, unique in three ways:

1. No book has ever challenged so many advertising industry attitudes, beliefs and practices.
2. This is the only book to ever identify and discuss the ten major problems in the industry.
3. The how-to part is based on an innovative approach to creating and evaluating advertising.

While there is no comparable book on the market, there are many books that look at advertising creativity and effectiveness. I consider those included here to be the most useful of the lot.

The Fall of Advertising and the Rise of PR (280 pages, Al Ries and Laura Ries, Harper Collins Publishers, Inc., 2002). Contains interesting, well-documented arguments for the superiority of PR over advertising for brand-building. Easy to read.

The New Account Manager (414 pages, Don Dickinson, The Copy Workshop, 2003). Smart and thorough, this is the definitive book on the overlooked subject of managing advertising accounts.

The Copy Workshop Workbook (439 pages, Bruce Bendinger, The Copy Workshop, 2003). Packed full of examples and how-to ideas, this is an excellent source of information and direction for creative types.

Bang (244 pages, Linda Kaplan Thayer, Currency, 2005). Lots of personal stories and some suggestions for making a big splash with your advertising. Received very mixed reviews. Thayer is not in the industry right now.

Ogilvy on Advertising (224 pages, David Ogilvy, Random House, Inc., 1985). Wisdom from one of the brightest minds in advertising history. Mostly how to do great ads. Includes some philosophies. The best known man and book in the industry.

Guerilla Advertising (283 pages, Jay Conrad Levinson, Houghton Mifflin Co., 1994). Primer on basic advertising for small businesses. Focuses on cost-effective strategies. In fifth printing.

How to Advertise (253 pages, Kenneth Roman, Jane Maas, with Martin Nisenholtz, St. Martin's Press, 2003) General how-to text book. First printing of Third Edition.

Advertising: Principles and Practice (640 pages, William D. Wells, John Burnett, Sandra E. Moriarty, Sandra Moriarty, Prentice Hall, 2003). Popular text book. Sixth edition.

Creative Advertising (266 pages, Mario Pricken, Thames and Hudson, 2002) Over 200 examples of international advertising, with ideas about the creative process and developing big ideas. 450 illustrations.

No-Copy Advertising (160 pages, Lazar Dzamic, RotoVision Publishing, 2001) Award-winning ads from around the world that contain no copy. They may or may not be effective ads, but this is a good place to see the power of demonstration.

Ordinary Advertising, and how to avoid it like the plague (204 pages, Mark Silveira, Xlibris Corporation, 2003). This book lays out the cardinal principals for doing extraordinary advertising that gets attention and makes a strong emotional connections with its audience.

Dynamics of International Advertising: Theoretical and Practical Perspectives (352 pages, Barbara Mueller, Peter Lang Publishing, 2004). With current examples and case studies, it addresses the key issues advertisers must keep in mind to create effective communication programs for foreign markets, such as cultural norms and values, political environments, economic policies, social contexts.

Confessions of an Advertising Man (224 pages, David Ogilvy, Southbank Publishing, 2004) Highly recommended for anyone involved in advertising, particularly copywriters. Ogilvy was a copywriter and he clearly has a special admiration for those who write copy for a living, but he also has great advice to share for anyone in advertising.

The Art of Writing Advertising: Conversations with Masters of the Craft: David Ogilvy, William Bernbach, Leo Burnett, Rosser Reeves (128 pages, Denis Higgins, McGraw-Hill, 2003) "What makes a great advertisement?" Nearly four decades ago, an unmatched group of five advertising pioneers first answered that question in *The Art of Writing Advertising*. Their entertaining and historically compelling answers still provide advertising professionals with valuable techniques for applying breakthrough creativity and innovation in the workplace.

The Copywriter's Handbook: A Step-by-Step Guide to Writing Copy That Sells (368 pages, Robert W. Bly, Owl Books, 1990) "This book succeeds on two levels. For beginners, it offers a clear, comprehensive guide to the business of and techniques used in advertising copywriting. And for the professionals behind the typewriter, this book is a valuable back-to-basics tool that should be given a prominent slot on the bookshelf."–*Los Angeles Times*.

Tested Advertising Methods (Prentice Hall Business Classics) (304 pages, John Caples, Fred E. Hahn, Prentice Hall, 1998) An excellent book on advertising writing by one of the great writers.

Advertising Secrets of the Written Word: The Ultimate Resource on How to Write Powerful Advertising Copy from One of America's Top Copywriters and Mail Order Entrepreneurs (312 pages, Joseph Sugarman, Delstar Publishing, 1998) Joe Sugarman sold a ton of merchandise with his direct response magazine ads, and he knows how to write advertising that gets results.

Cutting Edge Advertising II (424 pages, Jim Aitchison, Prentice Hall, 2003) Includes dozens of new print ads from the US, UK, Australia and Asia. For the first time, readers also get to see the latest work from the Philippines, South Africa, China and Eastern Europe.

How to Write a Good Advertisement (Victor O. Schwab, Wilshire Book Company, 1985) Though initially written in the early '60s, the concepts and approaches are still as smart and valid as the day they were written. A great source of knowledge on how to write ads.

Hey, Whipple, Squeeze This: A Guide to Creating Great Ads (288 pages, Luke Sullivan, Wiley, 2003) A guide for creating great ads. Sullivan provides pointers, tips, and guidelines on how to write and produce successful ads for all media. Second Edition.

The End of Advertising as We Know It (238, Sergio Zyman, Armin Brott, Wiley, 2002) This book talks to top management and marketing managers, telling them to require their ad agencies do effective work, and to focus on sales and results, not creative awards.

Advertising Today (512 pages, Warren Berger, Phaidon Press, 2004) An overview of the evolution of advertising around the world over the past 30 years, charting influences from the political and social upheavals of the 1960s, to the appropriation of cinematic production techniques and special effects in the 1980s, to the influence of the Internet in the 1990s.

Effective Advertising : Understanding When, How, and Why Advertising Works (216 pages, Gerard J. Tellis, SAGE Publications, 2003). It reviews and summarizes what we know today on when, how, and why advertising works. The primary focus of the book is on the instantaneous and carryover effects of advertising on consumer choice, sales, and market share. In addition, the book reviews research on the rich variety of ad appeals, and suggests which appeals work, and when, how, and why they work.

*Creative Leaps: 10 Lessons in Successful
Advertising Inspired at Saatchi & Saatchi*
(250 pages, Michael Newman, Wiley, 2003).
The book provides unique methodologies and
explores the transformational power of ideas.
It offers firsthand insights into the advertising
campaigns of Saatchi and Saatchi, revealing
the theories behind each campaign strategy, the
process behind creativity, and the behind-the-
scenes stories involved with each project.

*Brands & Advertising: How advertising
effectiveness influences brand equity* (400 pages,
Giep Franzen, et al, Admap Publications, 1999)
A comprehensive and critical examination of the
research methods available to help advertisers
and agencies develop more effective advertising.
It covers pre-testing, brand equity research,
market simulation and tracking. It also
explains the Advertising Response Matrix,
a new model that provides an overview of all
possible advertising responses and ways of
researching them.

Persuasion in Advertising (264 pages,
John O'Shaughnessy and Nicholas Jackson
O'Shaughnessy, Routledge, 2003). This book
explains how advertising works and sets out the
strategies for advertisers to adopt for persuasion.

The Ultimate Secrets of Advertising (256 pages,
John Philip Jones, SAGE Publications, 2001).
Andrew Fenning said, "John Philip Jones has
set himself the highest hurdle there is—how to
make advertising accountable. His argument
is precise, and his language entertaining and
intelligent, making this quest an essential,
provocative and delightfully enjoyable
voyage for professionals and students alike."

GLOSSARY

account manager/executive

The people in an ad agency who handle the planning, client contact and overall management of client accounts.

advertainment

Advertising that spends considerable effort to entertain readers or viewers, and little effort to deliver a product-oriented message.

advertiser

The organization whose product is the subject of an advertisement. The advertiser may use an advertising agency, freelance talent or internal creative personnel to create the advertisements.

advertising manager

The person in the advertiser's organization who has day-to-day responsibility for the advertising program, and who is usually the primary contact with their ad agency.

art director

The person on the creative team who has primary responsibility for design and visual elements of print projects. May also work on TV and audio-visual projects.

award shows

Creative competitions, sponsored by a variety of organizations and companies, that evaluate advertising entered, giving awards to those the judges deem the most "creative" by the judges.

big idea

The basic creative concept which guides development of an ad. It is the central theme or approach chosen to deliver the key message of the ad.

big promise

The most important promise an advertiser can make to their target audience. It should be, or be based on, the single most important benefit offered by the product. The big promise is the single most important thing an advertiser can say. Not to be confused with a tag line.

blind headline

A headline for a print ad, brochure or other written piece that gives no indication as to the advertiser or product, and doesn't contain a message. The objective of a blind headline is to make the reader read on in order to find out what the ad is about.

body copy

In print ads and other written matter, body copy is usually the smallest type size and largest number of words on the page. The job of the much larger headline and subhead is to draw the reader in to read the body copy, which should contain specific information to help the reader make a more informed purchase decision.

borrowed interest

Anything not directly related to the product being advertised that is used in a piece of advertising to command attention or in the presentation of the message. Common examples include fake news casts, celebrity spokespersons, reference to a holiday or special event, and analogous products or situations.

campaign

A coordinated advertising effort involving multiple media and activities that have a common creative concept, messaging and visual appearance.

clever

Things that entertain, fascinate or amaze us. Advertising is often called clever when it contains a play on words or humorous approach.

copywriter

The person on the creative team who has primary responsibility for writing copy. The copywriter collaborates with the art director to come up with concepts and develop them into finished ads.

creative

Advertising which creates a change in knowledge, beliefs or attitudes, leading to changes in behavior. Also refers to people who create things such as paintings, music, films or effective advertising. Often used as a noun to refer to the creative work itself (e.g. I like the creative.)

creative development research

Research conducted before and during the creative process, in an effort to provide information and direction to the advertiser and its agency's creative team.

creative director

The head of the creative team and the creative department. The CD is responsible for the quality of creative work, and supervises, trains and guides the art directors and copywriters on specific projects.

creative impact research

Research conducted after advertising has run in the media, to assess the impact the advertising had on the target audience. This is the accountability phase, where the advertiser tries to find out if the advertising was "effective," often by looking at sales results and what people thought of or remember about the ad.

creative philosophy

The sum of beliefs, attitudes and approaches a person has regarding the creation of advertising. Everyone has some form of creative philosophy, even if it isn't organized or even conscious. A creative philosophy provides the answer to such questions as, "What is good advertising, Is this an effective ad, What should an ad do, and What should an ad include?"

creative team

The basic creative team consists of an art director and a copywriter, working with and reporting to a creative director. In larger agencies and on larger projects, there may be multiple art directors and/or copywriters working on a project. Outside specialists such as illustrators, photographers and audio and video production personnel may be added temporarily to the creative team on a project basis.

demographics

Statistical information about an audience, including such factors as age, marital status, family size, education, income and employment.

double entendre

A phrase or sentence which can be taken to mean two different things.

effective

Able to do what a person or thing is supposed to do. Capable of carrying out a specific assigned mission.

emotional connection

Made when a reader, listener or viewer develops at least a moderately positive feeling toward a piece of advertising. This does not necessarily relate to the effectiveness of the advertising, but making an emotional connection with a person makes it more likely that the person will pay attention to, remember, and potentially take action on the advertising.

emotionalization

The use of only emotional information in an ad.

evaluative criteria

The factors that one uses to analyze and made judgements about the effectiveness of a piece of advertising. Things such as "I like this ad, This is creative, Wow, this is really clever and This is so funny" are not examples of specific criteria, only opinions.

focus group

A focus group usually includes 8-12 people from the desired target audience, gathered around a conference table at a research firm or other neutral location. Clients and agency personnel view them through a one-way mirror. A moderator shows pieces of advertising and leads the discussion. Participants get free food and non-alcoholic beverages, and are paid for their time.

infomercial

A form of television commercial that is typically as long as an entire 30-minute TV show. Infomercials usually follow a format which involves presenting a big promise, giving many reasons to believe the promise, testimonials of satisfied customers, and live product demonstrations.

internet and e-mail surveys

The research approach involves having people fill out surveys on their computer. The Internet and e-mail suffer from the inability to get totally accurate information because they do not allow the easy and rapid give-and-take of person-to-person interaction.

laboratory research

Groups of about 20-50 in size gather in a specially wired room at a research firm. They are shown advertising, usually TV spots, and asked to register their response by using an electronic device which often looks like a rheostat. A moderator usually shows pieces of advertising and leads the discussion. This method is good for identifying specific parts of the spot to which people strongly react.

mall intercept survey

People are "intercepted" while walking around the mall, asked to look at some advertising and answer questions about it. This is better than a phone survey because they actually see the advertising.

on-air survey

Ads are placed in regular TV or radio programming, then a phone survey is done to measure recall of the commercial and reactions to it.

onezies

Onezies are individual ads which don't look or sound like other ads from the same advertiser. They may use the same tag line, but are not otherwise similar. There is no consistent big idea, just a bunch of unconnected little ideas. The term onezie doesn't mean they run only once. It means the ad is one of a kind, not part of a coordinated, ongoing campaign.

paired comparison research

A research format in which two comparable cities or sets of cities are selected, a separate ad or ad series is run in each city, and the results of the two campaigns are compared to determine which campaign did the better job.

persuasion

This is the job of a coordinated marketing campaign – to change a person's mind, to convince them to change their beliefs, attitudes, habits and purchasing behavior.

phone survey

The research equivalent of telemarketing. Researchers call people, and if granted permission, they ask questions, generally several minutes worth.

psychographics

Qualitative factors of a social, political and personal nature used to describe and differentiate audiences. Includes such things as attitudes, preferences, likes and dislikes.

sampling error

Researchers add a caveat to statistical results, to reflect the fact that no two groups of research respondents can be truly equal. This is called sampling error. Instead of saying that "45% of respondents love the spot,", findings are reported with a " +/-" figure, usually 5%. This means that a 45% number could actually be as high as 50% or as low as 40%.

S.T.E.P. (Strategies and Tactics for Effective Persuasion)

A new creative philosophy which includes specific evaluative criteria, and which everyone can readily embrace and easily use. It replaces the usual I say-You say approach to creativity with a consistent direction, structure and focus.

tag line (slogan)

A short phrase or sentence which makes a statement about the advertiser or product. It is usually found under or near the advertiser's logo at the bottom of print materials.

teaser campaign

Usually done in print, TV or outdoor boards, a teaser campaign starts out with a visual, words or combination thereof that tells nothing about the product or advertiser. Over time, information or visuals are added until a complete ad is unveiled. The objective of a teaser campaign is to generate a feeling of anticipation and a desire to know what it's all about.

tone of voice

In advertising this means more than the tone of a person's voice. It includes everything that contributes to the feeling the ad gives. If the objective of a TV commercial is to stir patriotic feelings, such things as showing a waving flag, the national capital building or war heroes, playing the national anthem or the Marine Corps hymn and using James Earl Jones' deep, resonant voice, would all contribute to the patriotic tone of voice.

INDEX

Burnett, Leo
- quote on advertising's job, 11

Campaigns
- defined, 83, 181
- more effective than onezies, 84-85

Caples, John
- quote on long copy, 44

Certification, 111-112

Clever
- defined, 17, 181
- difference from creative, 17-20
- entertaining vs effective ad examples, 22-24

Client
- defined, 25-26
- ad approval by, 87-97

Competition
- mentioned in ads, 144-146

Cone, Fairfax
- quote, what is advertising, 20

Consumers
- advertising isn't giving anything to, 33
- attitudes toward advertising, 4
- hot buyers want to know, 46-47

Copy
- ad gurus quotes about long, 43-45
- body copy, 180
- hot buyers want it, 46-47
- infomercials prove value of information, 42

BOOK ORDER FORM

Give this thought-provoking and controversial book to your friends and colleagues. Order here.

[   ] YES. I want _____copies of the book
       Advertising: Industry in Peril.

Quantity	Price per book
1-2	$ 14.95
3-9	$ 12.95
10-49	$ 11.95
50-99	$ 10.95
100-499	$ 9.95
500+	$ 8.95

Add appropriate postage. See the postage calculator on the following page. Allow 3 weeks for delivery.

[   ] My check or money order for $_____is enclosed, payable to Olympian Publishing.

Please charge my: [   ] Visa   [   ] MasterCard
                  [   ] American Express

Name _____

Organization_____

Address_____

City/State/Zip_____

Phone_____ E-mail_____

Card #_____Exp. Date_____

Signature_____

Mail your order and payment to:

Olympian Publishing
13500 SW Pacific Highway, PMB 522
Tigard, OR 97223

POSTAGE AND PRICE CALCULATOR

Based on shipping all books to one destination. For other quantities and for international shipping, email john@johnmichelet.com with the number of books and delivery address.

USA

Quantity	Book Price +	Postage	= Total
1	$ 14.95	$ 3.95	$ 18.90
2	29.90	6.00	35.90
3	38.85	7.55	46.40
4	51.80	9.00	60.80
5	64.75	10.55	75.30
10	119.50	15.50	135.00
15	179.25	20.75	200.00
20	239.00	27.00	266.00
25	298.75	33.25	332.00
30	358.00	39.00	397.00
40	478.00	52.00	530.00
50	547.50	62.50	610.00
60	657.00	77.00	734.00
70	766.50	86.50	853.00
80	876.00	97.00	973.00
90	985.50	108.50	1,094.00
100	995.00	120.00	1,115.00
150	1,492.50	179.50	1,672.00
200	1,990.00	230.00	2,220.00
250	2,487.50	280.50	2,768.00
300	2,985.00	330.00	3,315.00
400	3,980.00	420.00	4,400.00
500	4,475.00	525.00	5,000.00
750	6,712.25	749.75	7,462.00
1,000	8,950.00	975.00	9,925.00

THE ZEPHYR AWARDS

The Zephyr Awards is an annual international advertising creative competition open to all advertisers, advertising agencies and free-lance creative personnel. It was founded by John Michelet, author of the book *Advertising: Industry in Peril.* Held each fall, judging is based on the persuasive power of the work.

The Zephyr Awards honor advertising that rises above the competition and the clutter, and makes a clear and powerful case for its product. Work is evaluated using specific criteria associated with advertising that is changing minds.

The Zephyr Advertising Awards judges ask themselves, "If I were in the market for this product, would this ad be strong enough to change my beliefs and attitudes, and make me more likely to purchase the product?"

For complete information about The Zephyr Awards visit www.zephyrawards.com. Contact The Zephyr Awards at service@zephyrawards.com.

ADVERTISING EFFECTIVENESS TRAINING

John Michelet, author of *Advertising: Industry in Peril*, spends much of his time on the road, bringing the message of effective advertising to organizations of all types.

To say that John Michelet is a dynamic speaker doesn't do him justice. He has a passion for advertising and for doing it right, a passion which is obvious as he captivates his audience with innovative and revolutionary thinking, delivered with intensity and clarity.

Through a variety of seminars and featured speaker engagements, he shares his knowledge, insights, philosophies and innovative advertising procedures with a variety of audiences.

Client	Service
Advertisers	• Ad program review & critique
	• In-house effectiveness training
Ad Agencies	• In-house effectiveness training
Media (Radio, TV, Cable, newsp., mag.)	• Seminars - clients and sales force
Conventions and Trade Shows	• Short seminars • Featured Speaker

John tailors his presentations to the needs and situations of his audiences. Here are some typical presentation titles:

- "Why most advertising is worthless.
  How to create some that isn't."
- "The 15 keys to creating effective advertising."
- "Developing a Smart Advertising Philosophy."
- "The Myth of Advertising Accountability."
- "Advertising: Industry in Peril"
- "The Shocking Truths about Advertising Effectiveness."
- "What every media salesperson should know about effective advertising."

Who Needs Advertising Effectiveness Training?

- **Anyone** who plans, creates, reviews and approves advertising.
- **Advertisers.** It's not enough to assume that your ad agency understands and creates advertising based on effectiveness principles.
- **Ad Agencies.** Advertisers assume that all agencies produce advertising that is effective. Unfortunately, most ad agencies don't understand the importance of using effectiveness principles, and don't even know what they are.

Advertisers of all sizes. Whatever the size of the advertising budget, all advertisers can benefit from doing effectiveness-based advertising. The cost of doing ineffective advertising is extremely high.

The Advertising Media. If you are a radio or TV station, a cable franchise, a newspaper or a magazine, the key to increasing your sales is not more sales training, it is advertising training.

Clients pay money to deliver their messages. If they feel advertising worked, they buy more. If they don't think it worked, they don't use the medium any more. Most media outlets don't understand a simple truth - Retaining clients isn't as much a matter of knowing selling than it is knowing advertising.

The biggest reason for advertising "not working" is very seldom because the media buy was bad. When advertising doesn't work, it is almost always because of bad ads.

The media teach their sales forces how to sell. Do they teach them enough about advertising to enable them to make your clients successful? No.

To be helpful to their ad agency and advertiser clients, media sales associates must know the difference between effective and ineffective ads, and be able to give some counsel on how to do effective advertising. When they help clients do smarter advertising, the clients will keep coming back?

Why Is Advertising Effectiveness Training Necessary?

One problem is that advertisers and advertising agencies, even many that are large and sophisticated, greatly underestimate the difficulty of changing a person's mind. As a result, they don't take the job of persuasion seriously enough and don't create ads capable of doing this difficult job.

What Is Special About These Presentations?

They contain new issues, new information, new ideas and new ways of looking at the whole business of advertising.

John Michelet has developed a unique, easy-to-use and reliable method of evaluating and assuring advertising effectiveness. He provides solutions and specific recommendations, not vague generalities.

His presentations contain the ideas, information and tools necessary to make career-enhancing changes for all attendees, whether they are from media outlets, advertisers or ad agencies. Experienced veterans will learn as much as the rookies.

Attendees will discover insights and solutions to crucial issues. John destroys closely-held beliefs and shoots holes in traditional "truths." He discards erroneous approaches and replaces them with brash new attitudes and profitable new ways of approaching creative challenges.

Highlights

Attendees come away from John Michelet's information-rich presentations with so many energizing new ideas, it may be hard to know what to implement first. It doesn't matter as long as you do something. Here are some of the issues covered:

- The ten fundamental problems plaguing advertising
- The surprisingly high cost of ineffective advertising
- The 15 secrets of truly persuasive advertising
- Why sales are not a measure of advertising success
- Why advertising doesn't have to get attention

- The reality about advertising accountability
- How to identify effective and useless advertising
- The difference between clever and creative
- How advertisers contribute to ineffective advertising
- Why humorous ads are often ineffective
- The one question every ad must answer
- Why a Big Promise is the key to success
- How to make believers of your audience

Complete information at
www.olympianpublishing.biz. or johnmichelet.com

NOTES